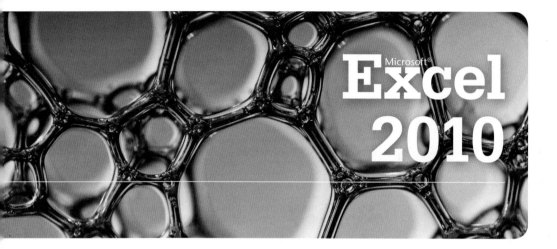

Microsoft®
Excel
2010

Prentice Hall
is an imprint of

PEARSON

Harlow, England • London • New York • Boston • San Francisco • Toronto • Sydney • Singapore • Hong Kong
Tokyo • Seoul • Taipei • New Delhi • Cape Town • Madrid • Mexico City • Amsterdam • Munich • Paris • Milan

PEARSON EDUCATION LIMITED

Edinburgh Gate
Harlow CM20 2JE
Tel: +44 (0)1279 623623
Fax: +44 (0)1279 431059
Website: www.pearsoned.co.uk

First published in Great Britain in 2010

Pearson Education is not responsible for the content of third party internet sites.

ISBN: 978-0-273-73613-4

British Library Cataloguing-in-Publication Data
A catalogue record for this book is available from the British Library

Library of Congress Cataloging-in-Publication Data
Holden, Greg.
  Excel 2010 Microsoft in simple steps / Greg Holden and Patti Short.-- 1st ed.
     p. cm.
  ISBN 978-0-273-73613-4 (pbk.)
 1. Microsoft Excel (Computer file) 2. Electronic spreadsheets. I. Short, Patti. II. Title.
  HF5548.4.M523H677 2010
  005.54--dc22
                            2010020896

10 9 8 7 6 5 4 3 2 1
14 13 12 11 10

Designed by pentacorbig, High Wycombe
Typeset in 11/14 pt ITC Stone Sans by 30
Printed and bound in Great Britain by Scotprint, Edinburgh

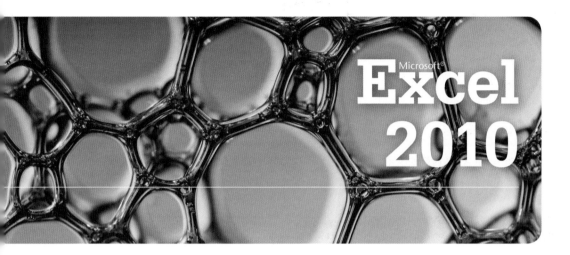

Microsoft®
Excel
2010

in **Simple**
steps

Greg Holden and Patti Short

Use your computer with confidence

Get to grips with practical computing tasks with minimal time, fuss and bother.

In Simple Steps guides guarantee immediate results. They tell you everything you need to know on a specific application; from the most essential tasks to master, to every activity you'll want to accomplish, through to solving the most common problems you'll encounter.

Helpful features

To build your confidence and help you to get the most out of your computer, practical hints, tips and shortcuts feature on every page:

ALERT: Explains and provides practical solutions to the most commonly encountered problems

HOT TIP: Time and effort saving shortcuts

SEE ALSO: Points you to other related tasks and information

DID YOU KNOW? Additional features to explore

WHAT DOES THIS MEAN?
Jargon and technical terms explained in plain English

Practical. Simple. Fast.

in Simple steps

Dedication:

To Peggy and our bright future together.

Author's acknowledgements:

Two teams help put together the *Simple Steps* books I've written. At home, I want to acknowledge the help of my assistant, Ann Lindner, and my co-author, Patti Short. In the UK, thanks to Steve Temblett, Katy Robinson and the rest of the Pearson staff for their help and support.

in Simple steps

Contents at a glance

9 Protecting and securing your data

10 Sharing your data with your colleagues

Top 10 Excel 2010 Problems Solved

Contents

Top 10 Excel 2010 Tips

1 Starting to use Excel

2 Learning essential workbook techniques

3 Managing workbooks and worksheets

4 Creating formulas and functions

5 Working with charts

6 Interpreting worksheet data with tables

7 Creating and modifying graphics and shapes

8 Publishing workbooks and worksheets

9 Protecting and securing your data

10 Sharing your data with your colleagues

Top 10 Excel 2010 Problems Solved

Top 10 Excel 2010 Tips

Tip 1: Launch Excel

Right from the start, Excel lets you do things your way. You can launch the application by selecting it from the Start menu. When the program starts, a blank workbook opens in a program window, and you can start working with it immediately.

1 On the Windows taskbar, click the Start button.

2 If you started the program recently, then select it from the list of recently used applications.

3 If the program is not on the Start menu, click All Programs.

4 Click Microsoft Office.

5 Click Microsoft Excel 2010.

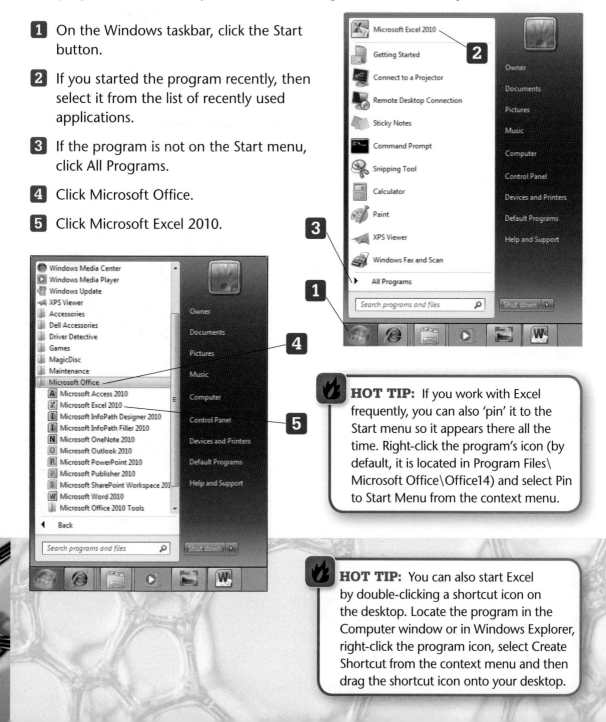

HOT TIP: If you work with Excel frequently, you can also 'pin' it to the Start menu so it appears there all the time. Right-click the program's icon (by default, it is located in Program Files\Microsoft Office\Office14) and select Pin to Start Menu from the context menu.

HOT TIP: You can also start Excel by double-clicking a shortcut icon on the desktop. Locate the program in the Computer window or in Windows Explorer, right-click the program icon, select Create Shortcut from the context menu and then drag the shortcut icon onto your desktop.

Tip 2: Select a cell

The whole point of having a cell is to do something with it: enter data in it, edit or move it, or perform an action in it. The first step is to select it so it becomes the active cell. But if you want to work with a group of cells, you need to first select them as a range. It's not necessary for them to be contiguous (adjacent to each other); they can be non-contiguous (in different parts of the worksheet).

1 To select a contiguous range of cells, click the first cell that you want to include in the range.

2 Drag the mouse to the last cell that you want to include in the range (or hold down the Shift key and then click the lower-right cell in the range instead of dragging).

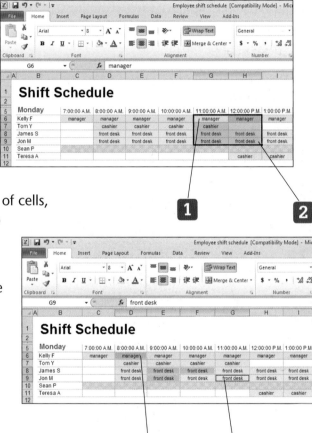

3 To select a non-contiguous range of cells, click the first cell that you want to include in the range.

4 Press and hold the Ctrl key while clicking the other cells or drag the point over the next group of cells you want to include in the range.

5 Repeat step 3 until all non-contiguous ranges are selected.

? DID YOU KNOW?

As you select a range, a range reference appears in the Name box located to the left of the formula bar. It contains the cell address of the top-left cell in the range, a colon and the cell address of the bottom-right cell in the range.

Tip 3: Select a worksheet

When you work with Excel, you store and analyse values on individual sections of workbooks called 'worksheets.' You can just call them 'sheets,' for short. The one you work on is the 'active' worksheet. Another name for it is the 'selected' worksheet. You'll be provided with a sheet tab, which is a concept that's like file folder labels. Selecting a worksheet is important because it enables you to apply formatting and other changes to the entire sheet at once. To select multiple worksheets, see 'Select multiple worksheets' in Chapter 2 for instructions.

1 Display other tabs if you need to by clicking the sheet scroll buttons.

2 Click a sheet tab to make the worksheet active.

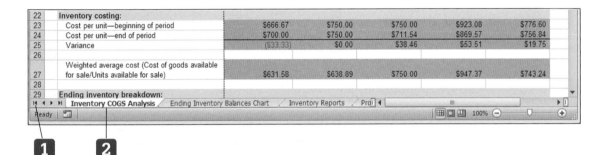

HOT TIP: You can select non-adjacent worksheets by pressing the Ctrl key while you click the next worksheet you want to include.

HOT TIP: You can select all the worksheets by right-clicking any sheet tab. Then click Select all sheets.

Tip 4: Create a basic formula

Formulas are powerful features of Excel worksheets. They calculate values you have entered and return results for you. Excel provides you with a set of operators that you can use to perform addition, multiplication, division and other calculations. Each formula starts with an argument: the cell references or values that combine to produce a result. If your formula gets too long, you can resize the formula bar to accommodate it.

1 Click the cell that you want to contain the formula.

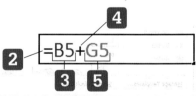

2 Type the equals sign (=) so Excel can calculate the values you enter. (If you don't, Excel will simply display what you type.)

3 Enter the first argument – a number or a cell reference.

4 Enter an operator such as the plus (+) for addition or asterisk (*) for multiplication.

5 Enter the next argument and repeat values and operators as needed.

6 Press Enter or click the Enter button (a tick) on the formula bar. The result appears in the cell.

Tip 5: Create a chart from all chart types

The general steps involved in creating a chart with Excel are outlined in 'Select the type of chart you need' in Chapter 5. As you can see there, it's a quick process. You can either create an embedded chart – a chart that is embedded in an existing worksheet – or one that is displayed on its own worksheet. If you open the Charts dialogue box launcher, you can select from among all the available chart types.

1 Select the data you want to present in the chart.

2 Click the Insert tab.

3 Click the Charts dialogue box launcher.

4 Click a chart category.

5 Select an option.

6 Click OK.

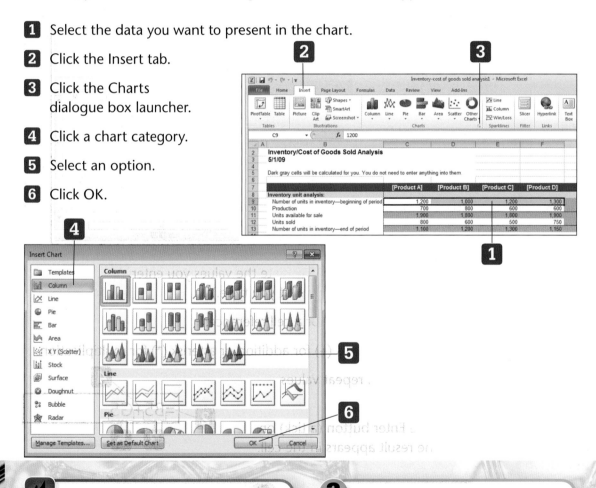

Tip 6: Create a table

In order to create a table, you first select the data you want to present, as you would any other feature. However, you need to make sure that that the field names are positioned in a single row in the first line of the list. In addition, each record in the table should be on a single row. Once you create the table, you can enter data directly in it, in any order; you'll learn how to sort the data in Chapter 6.

1 Open a blank worksheet.

2 Enter field labels on the first row of the table.

3 Type information for each record in a separate row.

4 Select all the cells in the table, including labels.

5 Do one of the following:

• Click the Table button on the Insert tab.

• Click the Format as Table button on the Home tab, and then select a table style.

6 Adjust the table size, tick the My table has headers box, and click OK.

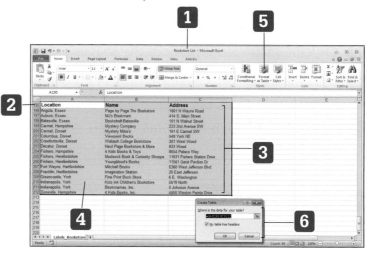

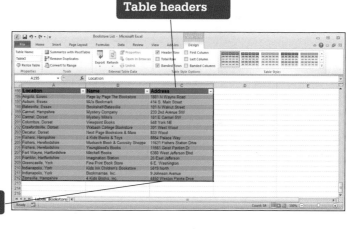

Table headers

Table data

HOT TIP: To delete a data table, select it and then press Delete to delete the entire table. If you want to keep the cells and just delete the data, click Clear and select Clear Contents.

ALERT: Make sure your table records do not contain any blank rows.

Tip 7: Draw a shape

You don't want to make your worksheets look unprofessional by drawing a clumsy or amateurish image atop your nicely arranged data. Excel helps by supplying ready-made shapes you can insert with a few mouse clicks and then edit as necessary.

1 Click the Insert tab.

2 Click the Shapes button.

3 Click the shape you want from the Shapes gallery.

4 Drag the cursor (which appears as a plus sign) down and to the right to draw the image.

5 Release the mouse button when you are done.

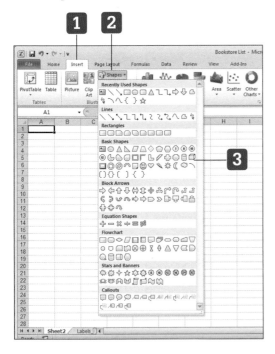

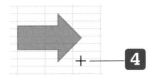

8

Tip 8: Configure page size and orientation

Before you print or otherwise publish an Excel worksheet, you need to set up the page size and orientation so it looks the way you want. You have the ability to change page orientation in Page Layout View. The Page Layout tab lets you adjust the page size quickly without opening a special dialogue box.

1 Click the Page Layout tab.

2 Click the Orientation button.

3 Select Portrait for vertically oriented printing or Landscape for horizontally oriented printing.

			[Product A]	[Product B]	[Product C]	[Product D]	Total
7			[Product A]	[Product B]	[Product C]	[Product D]	Total
8	**Inventory unit analysis:**						
9	Number of units in inventory—beginning of period		1,200	1,000	1,200	1,300	4,700
10	Production		700	800	600	600	2,700
11	Units available for sale		1,900	1,800	1,800	1,900	7,400
12	Units sold		800	600	500	750	2,650
13	Number of units in inventory—end of period		1,100	1,200	1,300	1,150	4,750
14							
15	**Cost of goods sold analysis:**						
16	Beginning inventory		$800,000	$750,000	$900,000	$1,200,000	$3,650,000
17	Add: purchases		400,000	400,000	450,000	600,000	1,850,000
18	Cost of goods available for sale		1,200,000	1,150,000	1,350,000	1,800,000	5,500,000
19	Less: ending inventory		770,000	900,000	925,000	1,000,000	3,595,000
20	Total cost of goods sold		$430,000	$250,000	$425,000	$800,000	$1,905,000
21							
22	**Inventory costing:**						
23	Cost per unit—beginning of period		$666.67	$750.00	$750.00	$923.08	$776.60
24	Cost per unit—end of period		$700.00	$750.00	$711.54	$869.57	$756.84
25	Variance		($33.33)	$0.00	$38.46	$53.51	$19.75
26							

? DID YOU KNOW?

The current page orientation is highlighted on the Orientation submenu.

? DID YOU KNOW?

You can print any comments you have added to files. Click the Page Layout tab. Click the Page Setup dialogue box launcher, click the Sheet tab, click the down arrow next to Comments, click As displayed on sheet or At end of sheet, and click Print.

Tip 9: Protect a worksheet

Passwords can be used to protect a worksheet. That way you won't have to worry about losing your hard work if others have access to your files. You're probably already familiar with the drill. You supply your password, and then you enter it again when you want to work on the file.

1 Click the Review tab.

2 Click the Protect Sheet button.

3 Select the check boxes for the options you want protected in the sheet or clear the check boxes for the options you don't want protected.

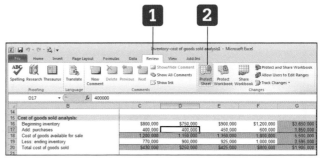

4 Type a password to prevent users from undoing your protection.

5 Click OK.

6 Retype the password.

7 Click OK.

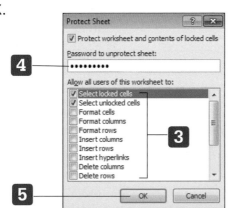

HOT TIP: Be sure to remember or write down your password(s), because you won't be able to open your files if you forget them. They are case sensitive, so you have to supply them exactly as they were first entered.

Tip 10: Share a worksheet

Collaboration takes on a new meaning when a group of people have equal responsibility for data within a single workbook. Sharing the Excel way means users can add columns and rows, enter data and change formatting.

1 Open the workbook you want to share.

2 Click the Review tab.

3 Click the Share Workbook button.

4 In the Share Workbook dialogue box, click the Editing tab.

5 Select the Allow changes by more than one user at the same time check box.

6 Click OK.

7 Click OK again to save your workbook.

HOT TIP: Maybe all team members are not created equal. Maybe one has veto control. Excel can keep track of changes, and the team leader can accept or reject them at a later date.

1 Starting to use Excel

Introduction

Congratulations for choosing Excel 2010 as your primary spreadsheet application for personal or business tasks that require manipulation of numbers. You won't see too much change from Excel 2007 to Excel 2010. In this release of Excel, improvements have been made to the accuracy of some of the mathmatical, financial and statistical functions. Even though the majority of features are carried over from Excel 2007, a few new features have been added here and there. One noticeable change that Excel 2007 users will notice is that the Office button, the big round button in the upper-left corner, has been replaced with the File tab on the ribbon.

Some of the new features added include a new version of Solver, Sparklines and the Slicer button. Additionally, Excel spreadsheets can now run in the web browser, where you can work with workbooks directly on the site where the workbook is stored. You can also share Excel via the browser with other users and set special permissions on who can access the document. Each new feature will be discussed in further detail in later chapters.

The ribbon has been improved in Excel 2010 so that you can create a personalised ribbon optimised to the way you work with the application. Customising the ribbon allows you to move and add controls to suit your needs. The customisation tools are accessible by right-clicking any tab on the ribbon and selecting Customize The Ribbon. An innovative feature called Sparklines has been added, which gives a visual snapshot image of a data trend over time within a cell. By using Sparklines you can insert similar graphic elements into selected cells. Additionally, a Slicer button has been added to increase the filtering of the data in PivotTables.

You don't need to be either an accountant or a computer whiz to get the most out of Excel. This book will show you step by step how to perform tasks either with a click of your mouse or with shortcut keys on your keyboard. You'll find the tools you need on a tab-based ribbon, on dialogue boxes or from context menus. And you can customise the quick access toolbar to get easy access to commands you use all the time. What's not to love?

This chapter introduces you to some of the basic functions you can perform with Excel, beginning with how to create those worksheets and make them into workbooks. You can use Excel's default setting and download templates, or you can create your own format for a specific project.

Launch Excel

Right from the start, Excel lets you do things your way. You can launch the application by selecting it from the Start menu. When the program starts, a blank workbook opens in a program window, and you can start working with it immediately.

1 On the Windows taskbar, click the Start button.

2 If you started the program recently, then select it from the list of recently used applications.

3 If the program is not on the Start menu, click All Programs.

4 Click Microsoft Office.

5 Click Microsoft Excel 2010.

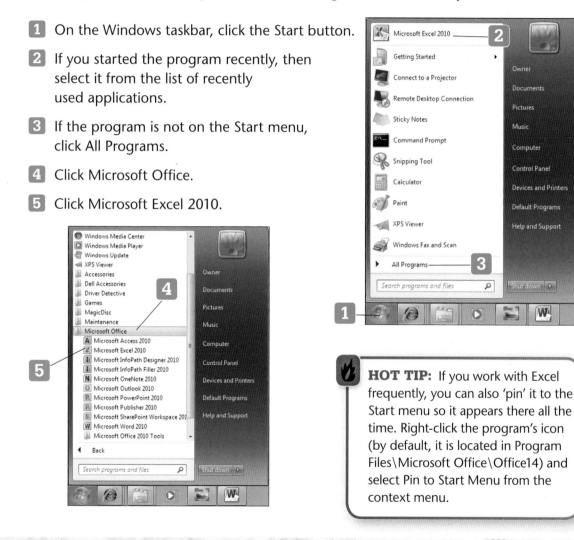

HOT TIP: If you work with Excel frequently, you can also 'pin' it to the Start menu so it appears there all the time. Right-click the program's icon (by default, it is located in Program Files\Microsoft Office\Office14) and select Pin to Start Menu from the context menu.

HOT TIP: You can also start Excel by double-clicking a shortcut icon on the desktop. Locate the program in the Computer window or in Windows Explorer, right-click the program icon, select Create Shortcut from the context menu and then drag the shortcut icon onto your desktop.

Create a new workbook

When you first start Excel, the application presents you with a blank workbook so you can immediately get to work. By default, three worksheets appear each time a new workbook is created. If you complete that workbook and save it, you can create another blank workbook at any time; you can create as many blank workbooks as you want, in fact. Each new file is given the generic name Book1, Book2, etc. until you save it.

1 Click the File tab.

2 Click New.

3 Click Blank workbook.

4 Click Create.

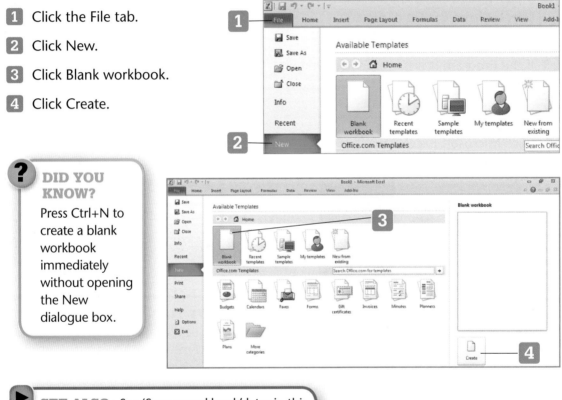

? DID YOU KNOW?

Press Ctrl+N to create a blank workbook immediately without opening the New dialogue box.

▶ SEE ALSO: See 'Save a workbook' later in this chapter for more on saving an Excel file.

? DID YOU KNOW?

You can increase or decrease the number of sheets that appear each time a new workbook is created. Go to the Excel Options dialogue box and modify the Include this many of sheets option. The minimum value is 1 and the maximum value is 255.

? DID YOU KNOW?

The information on the File tab is called Backstage View by Microsoft in its Help files. The name implies its purpose – to give you a glimpse behind the currently open document or program so you can change settings.

Create a workbook from a template

A template is an Excel workbook file that provides you with a unified work design. You'll get a professionally designed set of worksheets and themes, so you only need to add text and graphics.

1. Click the File tab.

2. Click New.

3. From Available Templates, select the template you want.

4. In the right pane, click Create or Download.

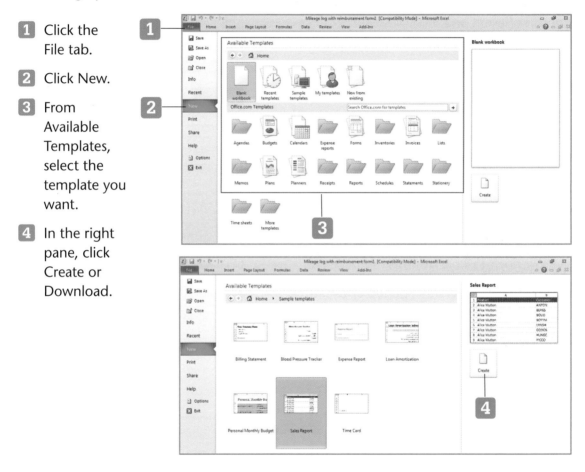

? DID YOU KNOW?

A template is a good thing to use when you have your content pretty much nailed but want the result to look professional.

🔥 HOT TIP: Templates are everywhere, just ripe for your picking. Go to www.microsoft.com, click the Office link, and then search for Excel Templates. You can pick them from a listed category. Or check out the Spotlight section in the Featured category, which you can set to automatically update. Or just stick to those already installed with Excel.

Open an existing workbook

You can open an existing workbook in one of two ways. You can double-click the icon for the workbook you want to open and, if Excel isn't running already, it will start up and open the file simultaneously. If Excel is already running then follow these steps as well:

1 Click the File tab.

2 Click Recent and a list of recent documents appear in the Recent Workbooks list.

3 If the workbook does not appear in the list, click Open.

4 If the file is located in another folder, click the Look in list arrow and then navigate to the file.

5 Click the file name to select it.

6 Click Open.

7 As an alternative, click the Start button on the Windows taskbar as usual.

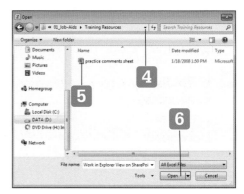

8 In the list of recently opened applications, select the arrow to the right of Microsoft Excel 2010 to expand the list of recent workbooks.

9 Click on the file name to open it.

HOT TIP: The Recent option on the File tab displays a list of files you've worked on recently, so you can work with them again at a moment's notice.

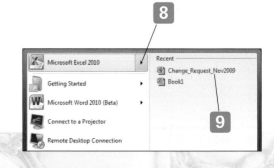

HOT TIP: If you want a specific file type, click the Files of type list arrow and take your pick.

? DID YOU KNOW?

Clicking the Pin icon next to the file name in the Recent Workbooks list pins the file to the list so it remains there until you click the Pin icon again to unpin it.

Explore the ribbon

You'll find the ribbon at the top of the workbook window. It's made up of tabs that are organised by tasks or objects. In turn, the controls on each tab are organised into groups or sub-tasks. The controls (or command buttons, if you prefer that term) in each group either execute a command or display a menu of commands or a drop-down gallery.

1 Click the tabs to access different sets of commands and options.

2 Look through the tool groups to find the individual command you want.

3 Click an icon or drop-down list to select a command.

4 To use the keyboard instead of the mouse to access commands on the ribbon, do any of the following:

- To display KeyTips over each feature in the current view, press and release the Alt or F10 key.

- Continue pressing until you come to the one you want to use.

- To cancel an action and hide the KeyTips, press and release the Alt or F10 key again.

HOT TIP: Do you want to see what your option change will look like before you commit to it? Point to a gallery option, such as WordArt, on the ribbon and you'll get a live preview.

DID YOU KNOW?

In Excel 2010, you can change the built-in tabs or create your own tabs and groups allowing you to personalise your workspace and access your favourite commands quicker. To customise the ribbon, right-click anywhere on it and select Customize The Ribbon.

DID YOU KNOW?

Excel automatically provides the three types of tab on the ribbon (standard, contextual and program) so you'll have whatever tools you might need based on what you're doing.

HOT TIP: To minimise the ribbon, double-click the name of the tab that is displayed, or click the Customize Quick Access Toolbar list arrow, and then click Minimize the Ribbon. Click a tab to auto display it (the ribbon remains minimised). To maximise the ribbon, double-click a tab.

Select menu commands

Excel commands are organised in groups on the ribbon, Office menu, quick access toolbar, and mini-toolbar. The Office button opens to display file-related menu commands, while the quick access toolbar and mini-toolbar display other buttons you'll use a lot.

1 Click the File tab.

2 Click the command you want.

3 If the command is followed by an arrow, point to the arrow to expand the list of related options. Then click the option you want.

4 You can right-click an object such as a cell or column header and select an option from the context menu.

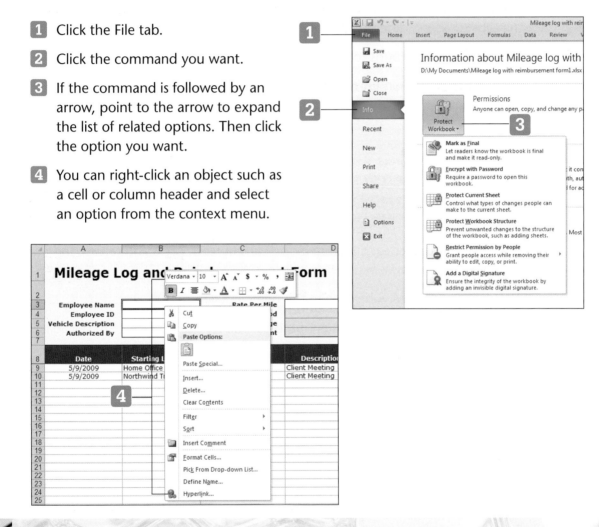

? DID YOU KNOW?

If you prefer keyboard commands, press Shift+F10 to display the shortcut menu for a selected command.

Work with the quick access toolbar

When Excel opens, you're provided with a set of its commonly used commands in the form of a quick access toolbar. The advantage of using the quick access toolbar is that it always remains on screen, no matter what tab you have chosen on the ribbon. You can also customise the toolbar so that it contains the commands you need most often. To add or remove a ribbon button or group, right-click the button or group name on the ribbon, and then click Add to (or Remove from) Quick Access Toolbar. Or do the following to customise:

1 Click the Customize Quick Access Toolbar list arrow.

2 Click More Commands.

3 In the Excel options Window, click the Choose commands from list arrow and select All Commands or a specific ribbon.

4 From the Customize Quick Access Toolbar list arrow and select the current workbook if you only want the commands to be available in the workbook. The For all documents (default) option adds the commands to all workbooks.

5 Click the command you want to add (left column) or remove (right column), and then click Add or Remove.

6 Click the Move Up and Move Down arrow buttons to arrange the order.

7 Click OK.

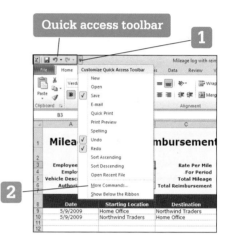

🔥 HOT TIP: To insert a separator line between buttons, click <Separator> from the list, and then click Add.

❓ DID YOU KNOW?

Excel displays the mini-toolbar when you point to selected text to give you quick access to formatting tools. It will appear above your selected text, but you can change that. Click the Customize Quick Access Toolbar list arrow, and then click Show Below the Ribbon or Show Above the Ribbon.

Select dialogue box options

Dialogue box launchers are small icons that appear at the bottom corner of some groups. If you click on one, a dialogue box will open. This allows you to supply more information before the program carries out the command you selected.

1 Click on a dialogue box launcher.

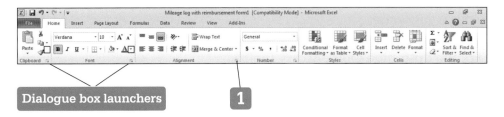

Dialogue box launchers

1

2 Enter information or make selections in the dialogue box.

3 Click OK to complete the command, or click Cancel to close the dialogue box without issuing the command. (If you see an Apply button, click it to apply your changes without closing the dialogue box.)

? DID YOU KNOW?

All dialogue boxes contain the same types of options. They include tables; option buttons; up and down arrows; and lots of boxes: check, list, text and preview.

HOT TIP: Rather than clicking to move around a dialogue box, you can press the Tab key to move from one box or button to the next. To move backward, use Shift+Tab. To move between dialogue box tabs, use Ctrl+Tab and Ctrl+Shift+Tab.

Use the status bar

If you look on the bottom of your screen, you'll see a status bar that displays workbook information and some controls. To customise exactly what you see there, you just need to click your mouse.

1 Right-click on the status bar, and then click on an option to select it. This adds the item to the status bar.

2 Right-click on the status bar, and then click on an item to clear the selection. This removes an item from the status bar

HOT TIP: In addition to displaying information, the status bar also allows you to check the on/off status of certain features.

Use task and window panes

Window panes are sections of a window, such as a split window. Task panes are sections of a window that appear when you need them.

1 Click a dialogue box launcher icon to open a task or window pane.

2 Close a task or window pane by clicking the Close button in the upper-right corner of the pane.

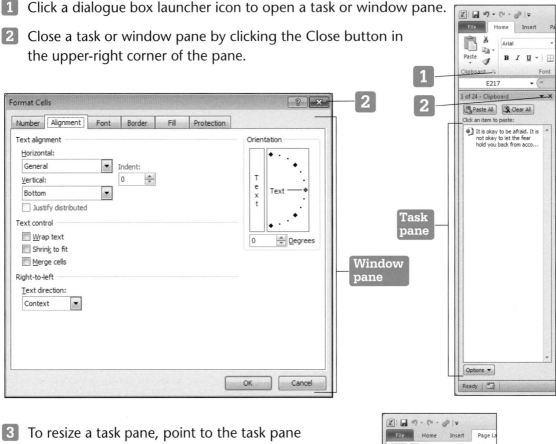

Window pane

Task pane

3 To resize a task pane, point to the task pane border edge until the pointer changes to double arrows. Then drag the edge.

Double arrow

HOT TIP: To insert window panes, click the View tab and then click the Split button in the Window group.

Navigate a workbook

Worksheets in Excel can be long and complex, and you'll save time by knowing all your options when it comes to navigating the document so you can find what you want. You can use your mouse or your keyboard to get around.

1 To move from one cell to another, point to the destination cell and click.

2 To move from one worksheet to another, click the tab of the sheet you want to jump to.

3 Click the sheet scroll buttons to view more sheet tabs.

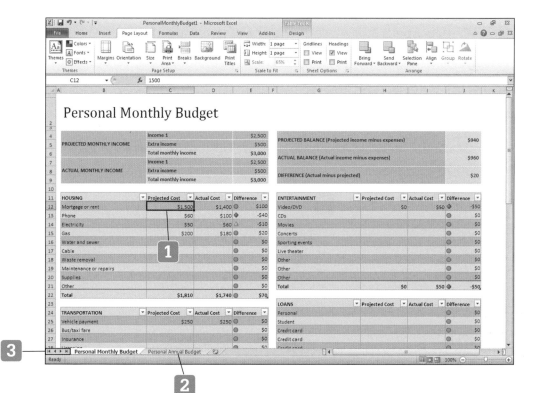

HOT TIP: You can jump to a specific location by clicking the Home tab, clicking the Find & Select button, and clicking Go To. Type the address of the cell you want and click OK.

Manage multiple windows

Each Excel workbook is contained within an individual window, which includes a title bar, status bar and the other familiar elements. Because your work can quickly become complex, you may well end up with three, four or more windows open on screen at once. Try these options for managing the windows so you can find them and work with their contents more quickly.

1 Open up the multiple workbooks you need to work with.

2 Click the View tab.

3 From the Window tool group, select one of the commands:

- New Window opens a new window containing a copy of the workbook.

- Arrange All arranges the multiple windows tiled, horizontal, vertical or cascade.

- Switch Windows lets you choose the name of the workbook you want in front.

- View Side by Side lets you view two files vertically at the same time.

4 Click the Maximise, Restore, Minimise or Close buttons to rearrange the currently active window.

Save a workbook

After you have been entering or editing data for a while (perhaps 15 minutes at the most), be sure to save it. That way you won't lose the changes you made before the last save. If you are saving a file for the first time, use the Save As command. If you are saving a file you have saved and named previously, click the Save button on the quick access toolbar.

1 Click the File tab.

2 Click Save As.

3 Click the Save in list arrow and select a location to save the file.

4 In the File name field, enter a name for the file.

5 From the Save as type drop-down list, select Excel Workbook.

6 Click Save.

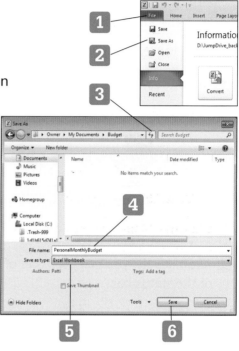

? DID YOU KNOW?

Excel makes it easy to save a file in different formats, such as earlier versions of Excel, so that users who don't have Excel 2010 can work with them. Another format you can save workbooks in is XML (Extensible Markup Language), a format that keeps file sizes small and provides improved file recovery options as well.

! ALERT: When you open a workbook that was saved as an earlier version of Excel, for example Excel 97–2003, it will open in Compatibility mode. Compatibility mode disables certain new features that previous versions of Excel cannot use.

? DID YOU KNOW?

By default, you save a workbook as an Excel 2010 document. Anyone who opens or wants to work with it needs to have Excel 2010 installed, or have downloaded a file conversion utility from the Web.

? DID YOU KNOW?

The Save As dialogue box also lets you select options such as Web (if you want to save the file as a webpage) or Compress Pictures.

Switch views

The View selector in the lower right-hand corner of the status bar lets you choose one of the common Excel views: Normal, Page Layout and Page Break Preview. Normal View is the default view in Excel, the one you're probably used to working with. Page Layout View is designed to give you a preview of how the file will look when printed out. Page Break Preview shows how your worksheet is broken into separate pages.

1 Click the View tab.

2 From the Workbook Views group, click one of the buttons: Normal, Page Layout, Page Break Preview, Custom Views or Full Screen.

3 Alternatively, you can click one of the View Selector buttons on the right-hand side of the status bar.

? DID YOU KNOW?

You can use Page Break Preview at the same time as Page Layout View.

Change workbook properties

While you work on a workbook Excel automatically saves any changes to the file's properties, such as its file size, its author, its subject and the last time it was saved. You can view or edit these properties at any time; you might want to identify yourself as the author, for instance, or create your own custom properties so you can track data more easily.

1 Click the File tab.

2 Click Info to display a list of options.

3 Click Properties.

4 Select Show Document Panel.

? DID YOU KNOW?

You also have the opportunity to protect the document with a password when you perform a Save As. In the Save As Dialogue box, click Tools and select General Properties.

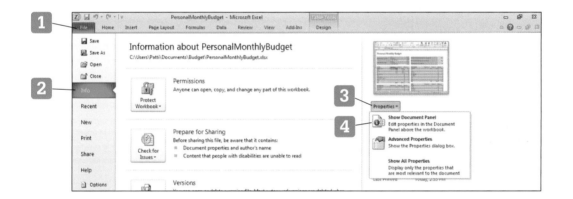

5 In the Document Properties view, enter information such as an author name, subject, keywords and a description.

6 When you're done, click the Close button on the Document Information Panel.

Find help while you're working

There are so many places to get help with Excel, you might need help just to access help to find them all. No matter which option you choose, a list of possible answers is shown to you with the most likely answer at the top.

1 On the Ribbon, click the Help button, or press F1.

2 Locate the Help topic you want by clicking on the Table of Contents button.

3 Alternatively, you can type a topic in the search field and press Enter.

4 Review the list of topic results and then click any links to get help information.

5 If desired, click the Print button on the toolbar.

6 Click the Close button.

5 **2**

Excel Help

ribbon | Search

Microsoft Excel Home

Search results for ribbon

3

◁ Back   Next ▶

Minimize the **ribbon**
ARTICLE | The ribbon is designed to help you quickly find the commands that you need to compl...

Commands on the **Ribbon** are disabled by the administrator
ARTICLE | Symptoms You try to use a command on the Ribbon, which is part of the Microsoft Off...

Commands on the **Ribbon** are disabled in Reduced Functionality Mode
ARTICLE | Symptoms You try to use a command on the Ribbon, which is a part of the Microsoft O...

Commands on the **Ribbon** are disabled because you don't have permission ...
ARTICLE | Symptoms You try to use a command on the Ribbon, which is part of the Microsoft Off...

Move the Quick Access Toolbar
ARTICLE | The Quick Access Toolbar is a customizable toolbar that contains a set of commands th...

Show the Developer tab
ARTICLE | The Developer tab is not displayed by default, but you can add it to the ribbon when y...

Make the switch to Excel 2010
TRAINING | Are you switching to Excel 2010 from a previous version? This course is for you?

Keyboard shortcuts in Excel 2010
ARTICLE | This article describes what Key Tips are and how you can use them to access the ribbon...

All Excel   Connected to Office.com

6

4

HOT TIP: There's also a Search button list arrow below the toolbar where you can select the location and type of information you want by typing keywords.

? DID YOU KNOW?
Without leaving the Help Viewer, you can use the web browser and ask questions. This will give you access to up-to-the-minute information.

Update Excel

Every application needs updates to fix features that don't work and provide new functionality. Excel makes it easy to find updated versions so you can improve the application, through the Excel Options dialogue box.

1 Click the File tab.

2 Click Help.

3 Under the Tools for Working With Office section, select Check for Updates to connect to the Microsoft Update website.

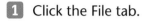

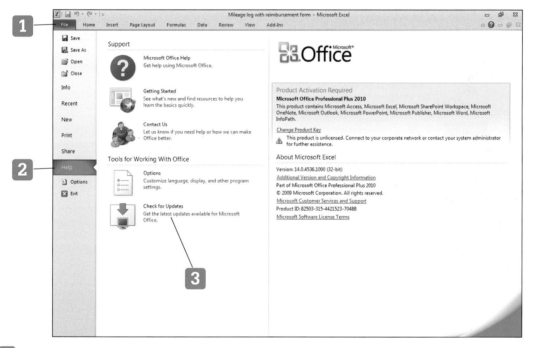

4 From the Microsoft Update website, select one of the update buttons to check your software to see if you need any Excel updates, and then select the updated files you need to download, and install them.

? DID YOU KNOW?

Updates are additions to software that can help prevent or fix problems, or improve how your computer works. Microsoft Update is a Microsoft website that scans your computer and gives you a list of updates relevant to your computer and its configuration. You decide what to download and install.

Close a workbook and quit Excel

After you finish making changes to a workbook, you can close it. Closing the file saves memory and unclutters your taskbar and desktop. Closing the file also ensures that you save changes. You can also quit the application, which also saves memory.

1 Click the File tab.

2 To close a workbook, click Close.

3 To quit Excel, click Exit.

4 Alternatively, you can click the Close (X) button at the top right-hand corner of the Excel window.

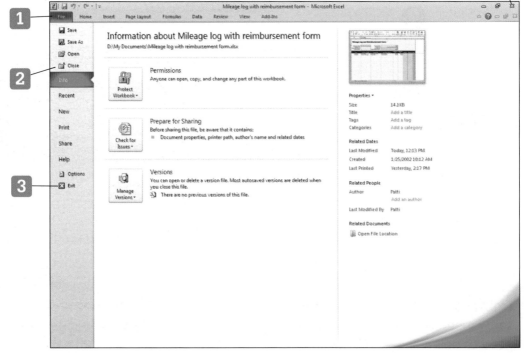

HOT TIP: Press Ctrl+Q to quit Excel (or another Office application).

HOT TIP: Press Ctrl+W to close a file. You will still be prompted to save changes first.

2 Learning essential workbook techniques

Introduction

The previous chapter helped you master the technique of entering data in the cells of an Excel worksheet. Now you're ready to start creating Microsoft Excel workbooks. The first thing you need to understand is that the address of the cell comes from it's column and row intersection. For example, C16 simply means you are in a cell located in the column labelled C in row 16. A cell can contain a number of things, such as a label, value or formula. The cell can also remain blank.

You can move between cells using the arrow keys or by simply clicking in the destination cell. Pressing the Enter key takes you to the next cell in the next row while pressing the Tab key takes you to the next cell in the next column. When you want to make a change, you'll use the Find and Replace feature. There are other research and language tools that can be helpful as you build your workbook.

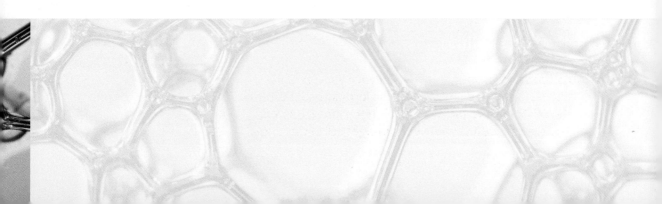

Select a cell

The whole point of having a cell is to do something with it: enter data in it, edit or move it, or perform an action in it. The first step is to select it so it becomes the active cell. But if you want to work with a group of cells, you need to first select them as a range. It's not necessary for them to be contiguous (adjacent to each other); they can be non-contiguous (in different parts of the worksheet).

1 To select a contiguous range of cells, click the first cell that you want to include in the range.

2 Drag the mouse to the last cell that you want to include in the range (or hold down the Shift key and then click the lower-right cell in the range instead of dragging).

3 To select a non-contiguous range of cells, click the first cell that you want to include in the range.

4 Press and hold the Ctrl key while clicking the other cells or drag the point over the next group of cells you want to include in the range.

5 Repeat step 3 until all non-contiguous ranges are selected.

? DID YOU KNOW?

As you select a range, a range reference appears in the Name box located to the left of the formula bar. It contains the cell address of the top-left cell in the range, a colon, and the cell address of the bottom-right cell in the range.

Select multiple rows or columns

Selection isn't limited to just cells in one worksheet. You may want to select rows or columns. Or even a range of cells across multiple worksheets. A lot of different types of data can be in a cell, for example, comments, constants, formulas or conditional formats.

1 If you need to select one row, select any cell on the row and press Shift+space bar. Alternatively, you can click the row header to select the row.

2 If you need to select one column, select the cell at the top of the column, and then press and hold the Ctrl+Shift+Down Arrow key combination. Alternatively, you can click the column header to select the column.

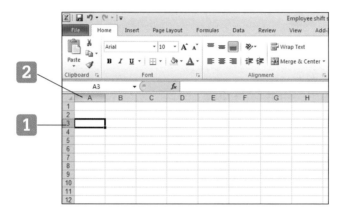

3 If you want to select contiguous rows or columns, click the row or column header, and then hold and drag your pointer along the row or column header.

Seven rows have been selected

? DID YOU KNOW?

When you click in a row or column header, the cursor turns into an arrow to indicate that you have selected the entire row or column.

4 If you want to select non-contiguous rows or columns, then press the Ctrl key while you click the rows or columns you want to include.

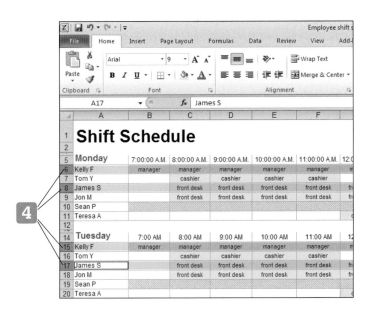

HOT TIP: To select contiguous rows or columns you can press and hold the Shift+Arrow key combination. Use the up and down arrow keys for rows and the left and right arrow keys for columns.

HOT TIP: To find what you're looking for, click Find & Select on the Home tab and select the Go To Special option.

Make special range selections

Once you select a range, you can refine or extend your selection. You can make a further selection of special cells within that range, for instance.

1 If you want to make a selection within a range, select the range you want. See the previous section for instructions.

2 Click the Home tab.

3 Click the Find & Select button.

4 Click Go To Special.

5 In the Go To Special dialogue box, select the option in which you want to make a selection. If you select the Formulas option, select or clear any of the formula-related check boxes.

6 Click OK.

HOT TIP: If you want to select cells with formulas that refer to the active cell, select the Dependents option. Or to select cells that are different from other cells in a row or column, select the Row Differences or Column Differences option.

DID YOU KNOW?

Excel will display a message for you if it can't find any cells that match your selection.

Select multiple worksheets

Many times you will be required to work with multiple worksheets. Excel lets you select contiguous and non-contiguous worksheets. You can group worksheets by selecting multiple sheets. Additionally, you can format or print a selection of sheets at the same time.

1 If you want to select contiguous worksheets, press Shift and click the last worksheet tab you want to include.

1

29	Ending inventory breakdown:

Inventory COGS Analysis / Ending Inventory Balances Chart / Inventory Reports / Product List

Ready

2 If you want to select non-contiguous worksheets, press Ctrl and click the next worksheet(s) you want to include.

3

3 When you make a worksheet selection (either contiguous or non-contiguous), Excel enters Group mode. To get out of Group mode, right-click on any worksheet tab and select Ungroup Sheets.

2

Enter a label

Labels transform a worksheet full of numbers into a meaningful report. They describe the data in worksheet cells, columns and rows.

1 To enter a text label, click a cell and type your label. Press Enter or press the Tab key when you have finished.

2 Alternatively, you can click a cell and type a label on the formula bar. Press Enter when you have finished.

3 To enter a number as a label, click a cell and type an apostrophe and then a number value. Press Enter or press the Tab key when you have finished.

4 Alternatively, you can click a cell and type a label on the formula bar. Press Enter when you have finished.

? DID YOU KNOW?

Don't worry when you type that apostrophe on a number label. It's just a label prefix that won't appear on the worksheet. Its purpose is to keep Excel from using the number in its calculations.

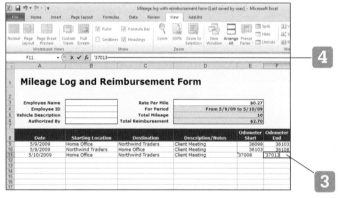

🔥 HOT TIP: Using Excel's AutoComplete feature will keep your labels consistent, but you can't use it for numbers, dates or times. It automatically completes your entries based on labels you've done before. If you don't like what it comes up with at first, just keep typing; otherwise press Enter.

Enter a value

A value can be a whole number, decimal, percentage or date. You can enter it using the numbers on the top row of your keyboard or by pressing your Num Lock key, which allows you to use the numeric keypad on the right.

1 To enter a value, click a cell and type a value. Press Enter or press the Tab key when you have finished.

2 Alternatively, you can click a cell and type a value on the formula bar. Press Enter when you have finished.

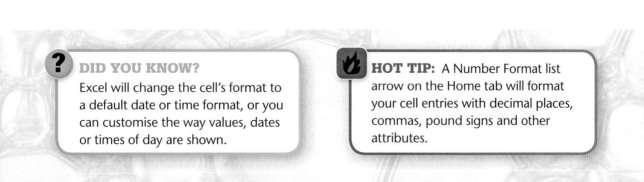

? DID YOU KNOW?

Excel will change the cell's format to a default date or time format, or you can customise the way values, dates or times of day are shown.

🔥 HOT TIP: A Number Format list arrow on the Home tab will format your cell entries with decimal places, commas, pound signs and other attributes.

3 To enter a date or time, click a cell and type a date by using a slash or hyphen between the month, day and year in the cell or on the formula bar. Press Enter or press the Tab key when you have finished.

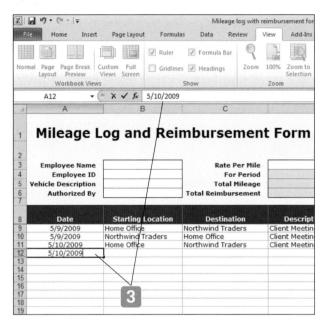

4 Click a cell or on the formula bar and then type an hour based on the 12-hour clock, followed by a colon, followed by the minute, followed by a space, and ending with an 'a' (for a.m.) or a 'p' (for p.m.). Press Enter or press the Tab key when you have finished.

HOT TIP: To simplify your data entries you don't need to type '10.00'; just '10' will do.

Enter data using AutoFill

One of the quickest and easiest options for entering data in worksheets is to let Excel do the work for you. AutoFill is an Excel feature that automatically fills in data based on the data in adjacent cells. You access AutoFill by clicking and dragging the fill handle, the little black triangle at the bottom right corner of a cell. AutoFill is perfect when you want to fill out a sequence of numbers, such as a set of numbers from 1 to 100, without having to type each one individually.

1 Click a cell and type the starting value. This cell's contents will determine how other cells are filled.

2 Position the mouse pointer over the lower right corner of the cell. The pointer changes to a black plus sign called a fill handle.

3 Click and drag the fill handle over the range of cells you want to fill, and release the mouse button when you are done.

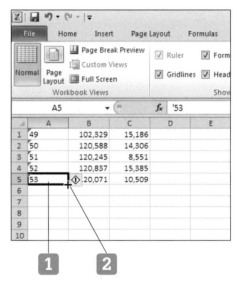

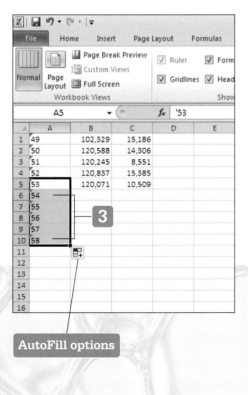

AutoFill options

? DID YOU KNOW?

The AutoFill menu will appear whenever something is pasted into a cell or you perform a fill operation. The options provided are limited by the data you are manipulating, so if you are working with dates you will see the date AutoFill options.

Insert or delete cells

Did you forget to enter some data? No problem. When you add more cells, those that were already there in a column or row will move in any direction you want. Or maybe you've decided against keeping cells. The opposite happens then. Cells that are left behind will move to the left or up. To insert a cell, follow these steps:

1 Select the cell or cells where you want to insert new ones.

2 Click the Home tab.

3 Click the Insert or Delete button arrow.

4 Select Insert Cells or Delete Cells.

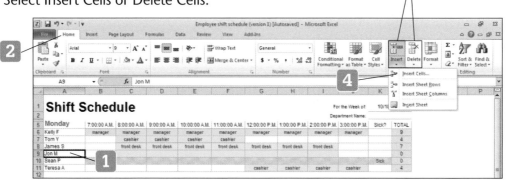

5 In the Insert or Delete dialogue box, select the option you want. Their names describe what they do.

6 Click OK.

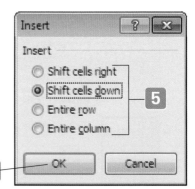

? DID YOU KNOW?

Keep in mind that when you delete a cell, Excel will remove the actual cell from the worksheet. But when you add a cell, Excel will adjust any formulas so they will refer to the right ones.

? DID YOU KNOW?

Don't confuse deleting with clearing. Deleting means the cells are totally gone from the worksheet. But clearing removes only the cell's contents or its format (or both).

🔥 HOT TIP: If you want to insert cells to the right and be quick about it, click the Insert Cells button on the Home tab.

🔥 HOT TIP: You can also right-click on a cell to select the insert and delete options.

Clear cell contents

Clearing a cell is a way of removing the data from it without actually deleting the cell from the worksheet. You have the option to clear whatever contents you specify: notes, data, comments or formatting.

1 Select the cell or cells you want to clear.

2 Click the Home tab.

3 From the Editing tool group, click the Clear button and select one of the following:

- Clear All clears the contents and formatting.
- Clear Formats leaves the contents but removes formatting.
- Clear Contents leaves the formatting but removes the contents.
- Clear Comments deletes any comments.
- Clear Hyperlinks deletes any hyperlinks.

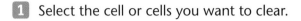

HOT TIP: You can quickly clear a cell's content by right-clicking the cell and selecting Clear Contents from the context menu.

Find cell contents

The steps for finding cell contents are pretty similar for finding and replacing content. Finding, for example, is if you need to find each figure in a long report to make sure the correct graphic is there. Whereas replacing is if you want to replace all references to cell D4 in Excel formulas with cell K2.

1 Click at the beginning of the worksheet.

2 Click the Home tab.

3 Click the Find & Select button.

4 From the drop-down list, click Find.

5 In the Find and Replace dialogue box, enter the text you want to find.

6 Click the Find Next button until the text you want to locate is selected. If a message box appears when you reach the end of the worksheet, click OK.

7 Click Close.

HOT TIP: Pressing the Ctrl+F key combination displays the Find and Replace dialogue box with the Find tab displayed.

HOT TIP: Go ahead and click Find Next as much as you like. No replacement will be made that you don't want.

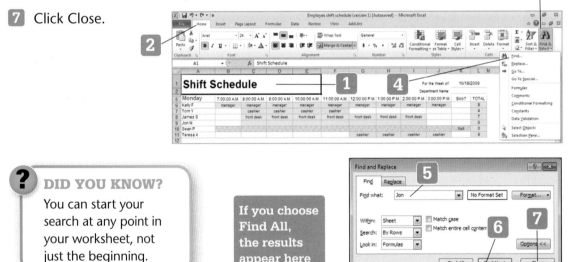

DID YOU KNOW?

You can start your search at any point in your worksheet, not just the beginning.

If you choose Find All, the results appear here

DID YOU KNOW?

You can click the Options button in the Find and Replace dialogue box to further define your search. For example, if you want to find cells that just match specific content across all the worksheets, then select Workbook from the Within drop-down list.

Replace cell contents

In order to replace cell contents, you use the same dialogue box that you use for finding content. Just click the Replace tab. You are presented with two data entry boxes: Find what and Replace with. Enter the appropriate content in each dialogue box, and then replace content individually each time it is found or globally by using the Replace All command.

1 Click at the beginning of the worksheet.

2 Click the Home tab.

3 Click the Find & Select button.

4 From the drop-down list, click Replace.

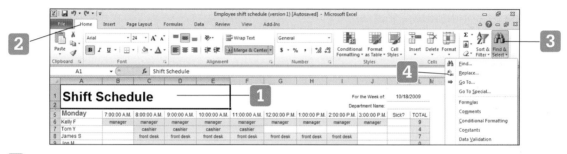

5 In the Find what text field, enter the text you want to find.

6 In the Replace with text field, enter the text you want to replace the text found.

7 Click the Find Next button until the text you want to replace is located.

8 Click the Replace button to replace the text found, or click the Replace All button to replace all instances of the text throughout the entire worksheet. If a message box opens when you reach the end of the worksheet, click OK.

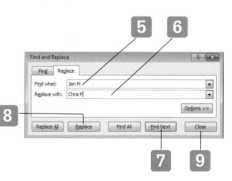

9 Click Close.

🔥 **HOT TIP:** Pressing the Ctrl+H key combination displays the Find and Replace dialogue box with the Replace tab displayed.

❓ **DID YOU KNOW?**

The Find and Replace dialogue boxes are a little different from one Office program to the next, but all commands are pretty similar in the way they work.

Move cell contents using the Clipboard

Copied data stays at its original location as well as being added to the new location. But there are several ways to move data without having to retype it. You can cut and paste directly, or you can store cell or range content on a Clipboard until you decide what to do with it next. Or you can use the drag-and-drop feature. In each case, you start out by selecting what you want to move.

1 Begin by selecting the cells that contain the data you want to move. The cells being moved must be contiguous – that is, adjacent to each other.

2 Click the Home tab.

3 Click the Cut button (the scissors icon). You'll get an outline of the selected cells called a marquee

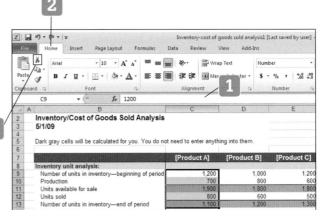

that shows the size of the selection. If you don't want to paste this information, press the Esc key to make the marquee go away.

4 Click the top left cell of the range where you want to paste the data.

5 Click the Paste button.

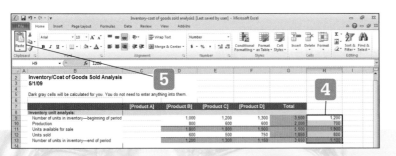

? DID YOU KNOW?

When you copy multiple items to the Office Clipboard, the last item you copy is always copied to the system Clipboard. You can paste items from the Office Clipboard individually, or all at once.

🔥 HOT TIP: Press the Ctrl+X key combination to cut the cell range and place it onto the Clipboard. Press the Ctrl+V key combination to paste the cell range from the Clipboard.

? DID YOU KNOW?

Although the marquee disappears, the data will stay on the Clipboard until you paste it somewhere or replace it with another selection.

Move data using drag-and-drop

If you're more at ease using your mouse to manipulate objects on screen rather than using keyboard shortcuts or menu commands, you can use drag-and-drop to quickly move data.

1 Select the cell or cells that contain the data you want to move.

2 Click the Cut button (the scissors icon). You'll get an outline of the selected cells called a marquee that shows the size of the selection.

3 Move the mouse pointer to the edge of the cell until the pointer changes to an arrowhead.

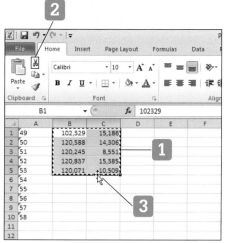

4 Press and hold the mouse button while dragging the selection to its new location, and then release the mouse button.

Check your spelling

It's just as important to have error-free text on a worksheet as on an essay. You might even say it's trickier because you're more likely to have technical terms, acronyms or made-up words that are unique to your company. Excel has a number of features to meet your needs, but the basic way to spell check will probably be familiar to you.

1 Click the Review tab.

2 In the Proofing tool group, click the Spelling button.

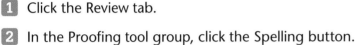

3 Excel will prompt you to make corrections. Choose a suggestion and click the Change button.

4 Click Close.

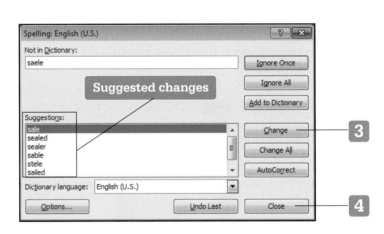

HOT TIP: If Excel does not find any spelling errors, a message appears telling you that you've completed the spell check.

DID YOU KNOW?

The AutoCorrect feature automatically corrects words as you type. When you're doing your spelling check, you can select a correct word and then click the AutoCorrect button to add it to the AutoCorrect list.

DID YOU KNOW?

Typical words are included in Excel's dictionary, but you can click the Add to Dictionary button so additional words won't show up as misspelled words in future.

Translate text

If you need to translate single words or short phrases into a different language, you can use the Research task pane. The first time you use translation services, you need to click OK under the Translate button to install the bilingual dictionaries and enable the service.

1 Select the text you need to translate.

2 Click the Review tab.

3 Click the Translate button.

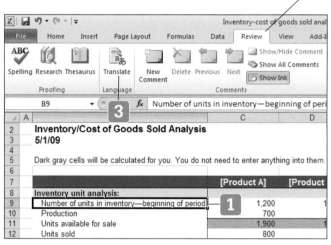

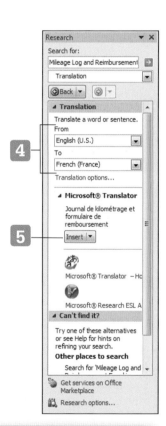

4 In the Research task pane, select a language from the From and To drop-down lists. By default, the From selection will be your default language, such as English.

5 Click the Insert button.

? DID YOU KNOW?

If you need to translate an entire document for basic subject matter understanding, you can use a web-based translation service. Just keep in mind that although that might be helpful for general meaning, the full meaning may not be preserved.

? DID YOU KNOW?

If English is your second language, the English Assistant is a Microsoft Office Online service that might help you write professional text. It will help you with spelling, explanation, usage, synonyms and related example sentences.

Change proofing options

Excel and Office have the ability to spell check a document automatically, but it's a good idea to adjust the proofing options first. The proofing options, which apply to all Office programs, give you the option to ignore web addresses and other words, for instance.

1 Click the File tab.

2 Click Options.

3 Click Proofing.

4 Select or clear the options you want.

5 Click OK.

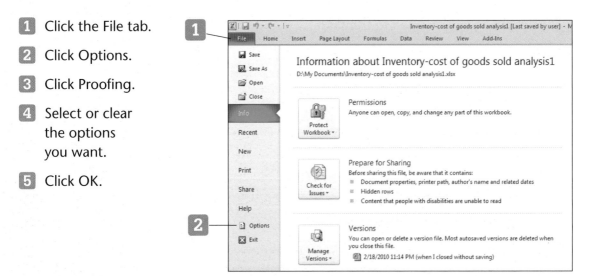

? DID YOU KNOW?

While you are editing a workbook, you can set options that let the spelling checker search for mistakes in the background.

3 Managing workbooks and worksheets

Introduction

The previous chapters helped you master the technique of entering data into cells, creating workbooks, and selecting a range of cells, rows and columns. Now you're ready to modify your workbook by adding, deleting and moving worksheets. You can even rename your worksheets if the focus of your workbook changes. Perhaps you want to protect certain data and hide those worksheets within your workbook. If you have a long list of data in a worksheet, you can freeze specific columns and row headers.

Whenever you modify a worksheet with formulas, Excel will recalculate those formulas accordingly. So you never have to worry about your results being out of date. Cell references will automatically be updated in the existing formulas. Plus, you can insert and delete cells, rows and columns, and you can adjust column width and row height so the worksheet will be correctly structured to suit your preferences.

Select a worksheet

When you work with Excel, you store and analyse values on individual sections of workbooks called 'worksheets'. You can just call them 'sheets', for short. The one you work on is the 'active' worksheet. Another name for it is the 'selected' worksheet. You'll be provided with a sheet tab, which is a concept that's like file folder labels. Selecting a worksheet is important because it enables you to apply formatting and other changes to the entire sheet at once. To select multiple worksheets, see 'Select multiple Worksheets' in the previous chapter for instructions.

1 Display other tabs if you need to by clicking the sheet scroll buttons.

2 Click a sheet tab to make the worksheet active.

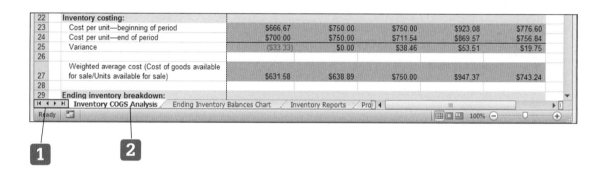

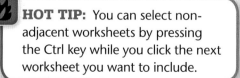

HOT TIP: You can select all the worksheets by right-clicking any sheet tab. Then click Select all sheets.

HOT TIP: You can select non-adjacent worksheets by pressing the Ctrl key while you click the next worksheet you want to include.

Name or rename a worksheet

The sheet names, by default, are Sheet1, Sheet2 and Sheet3. But you should choose a name for your worksheet when you create it so that you can remember what's in it. That way, you'll know which sheet to choose when you're faced with multiple sheets within a workbook.

1 Double-click on one of the existing worksheet tabs. Alternatively, you can click the Home tab, click the Format button, and then select Rename sheet from the drop-down list.

2 Enter the new name of the worksheet and press Enter.

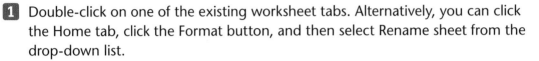

HOT TIP: You can also rename a worksheet by right-clicking on the tab and selecting Rename from the context menu.

DID YOU KNOW?

If you need more than three worksheets for your project, add them now so that you'll have all the information you need for your project in one file.

DID YOU KNOW?

The maximum length for a tab is 31 characters.

HOT TIP: To see most of the sheets within a workbook, you should pick short names for each sheet. That's because the sheet tab will get longer to accommodate the size of the name.

Move a worksheet

When you're ready to reorganise sheets in a workbook, you can arrange them in chronological order or you can place the most important one first. It's easy to move or copy a sheet within a workbook or to a different open workbook

1 Find the worksheet you want to move and click its sheet tab. Next hold down the mouse button.

2 The mouse pointer changes into an icon that resembles a sheet of paper.

3 Drag it to where you want to move the worksheet, and then release the mouse button.

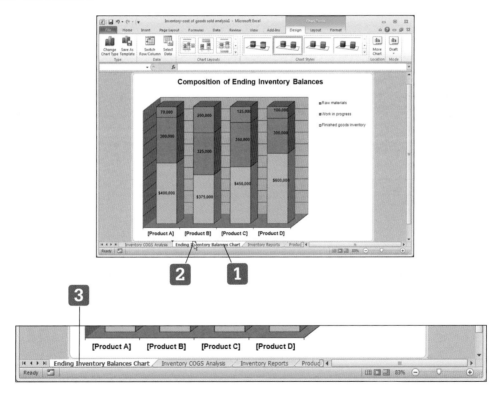

Copy a worksheet

If you need to re-enter data contained on one sheet in another sheet, you can always retype it. But this is time-consuming and introduces the possibility of typing errors. It's far easier and more efficient to copy the entire worksheet.

1 Find the worksheet, or group of worksheets, you want to copy and click its sheet tab.

2 Click the Home tab.

3 Click the Format button.

4 Select Move or Copy Sheet from the drop-down list.

5 In the Before sheet list box, select a sheet where the new copy will appear.

6 Alternatively, you can select the (move to end) option to create the new copy at the end of the workbook.

7 Click the Create a copy option.

8 Click OK.

5

6

7

8

Move or Copy

Move selected sheets
To book:

Employee shift schedule.xlsx

Before sheet:

Shift Schedule
Shift Schedule - February
Shift Schedule - March
(move to end)

☐ Create a copy

OK   Cancel

? **DID YOU KNOW?**

It's easier to copy a worksheet than to re-enter similar information on a new sheet.

? **DID YOU KNOW?**

If you need to copy a sheet to another workbook, select the workbook from the To book drop-down list.

? **DID YOU KNOW?**

You can use the mouse to move or copy a worksheet a short distance. If you have multiple sheets within a workbook, it's faster and easier to use the Move or Copy command to move a single sheet.

Insert a column or row

You don't have to redo the whole spreadsheet if you left out a row or column. Inserting a new row or column won't disturb your worksheet between existing data. To accommodate new columns and rows, Excel repositions existing cells and maintains formula calculations. Columns are inserted to the left; rows are inserted above the selected row.

1 To insert a new column, select the column where you want to insert a new one.

2 Click the Home tab.

3 Click the Insert button.

4 Select Insert Sheet Columns from the drop-down list. A new column appears to the left of the selected column.

HOT TIP: You can also right-click the selected row or column and then select Insert on the context menu.

ALERT: When you insert rows or columns, the maximum size of a worksheet is 65,536 rows by 256 columns.

5 To insert a new row, select the row where you want to insert a new one.

6 Click the Home tab.

7 Click the Insert button.

8 Select Insert Sheet Rows from the drop-down list. A new row appears above the selected row.

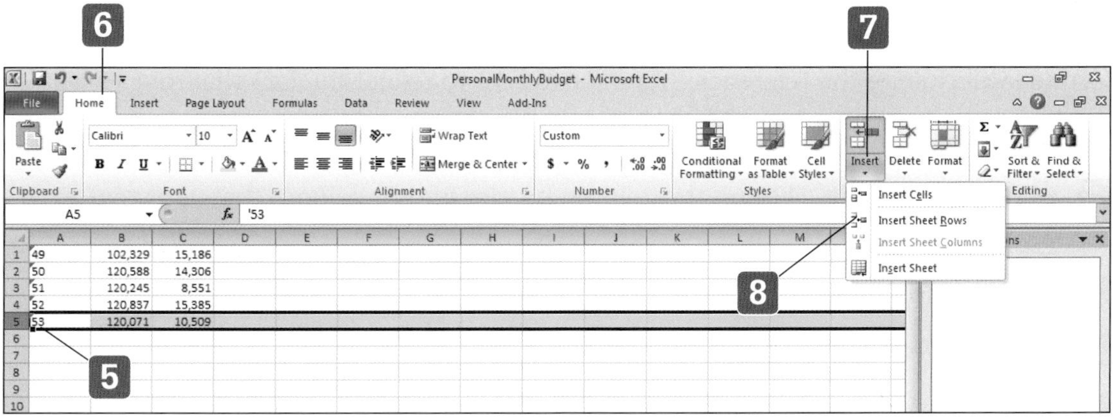

9 To adjust formatting, click the Insert Options button and then select a formatting option.

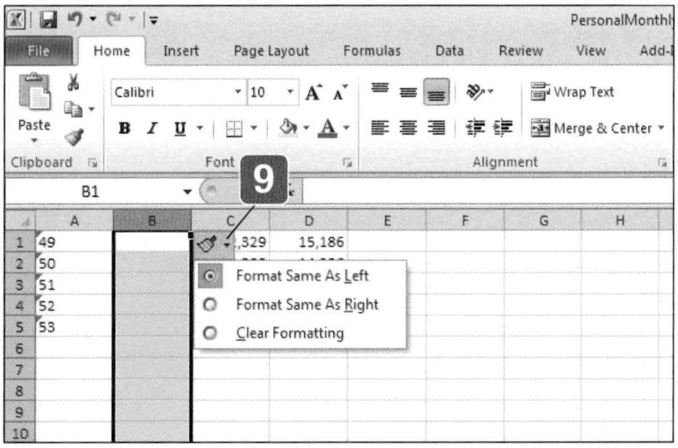

HOT TIP: To repeat the action of inserting a column or a row, click the location where you want to insert the column or row, and then press the Ctrl+Y key combination.

Delete a column or row

When you have data in a row or a column that is no longer needed, then deleting a column or row helps you focus on the data you really need. It also makes an entire worksheet easier to read on screen. When you delete a row or column, adjacent rows or columns move up or to the left to join the remaining data. When you delete columns or rows, the cell references in functions and formulas will usually update automatically. For example, if you have reference cell D11 in a formula and later add a row above this, the formula will change the reference from D11 to D12 to reflect the fact that row 11 was pushed down to become row 12 once the new row was added.

1 To delete a column, click on the column header for the column that you want to delete.

2 Click the Home tab.

3 Click the Delete button.

4 Select Delete Sheet Columns from the drop-down list.

HOT TIP: You can delete multiple columns and rows (adjacent or non-adjacent) by pressing and holding the Ctrl key while selecting the columns and rows you want to delete. Once finished selecting the columns and rows to be deleted, press the Delete key or right-click a row or column header and select Delete from the context menu.

5 To delete a row, click the row header for the row that you want to delete.

6 Click the Home tab.

7 Click the Delete button.

8 Select Delete Sheet Rows from the drop-down list.

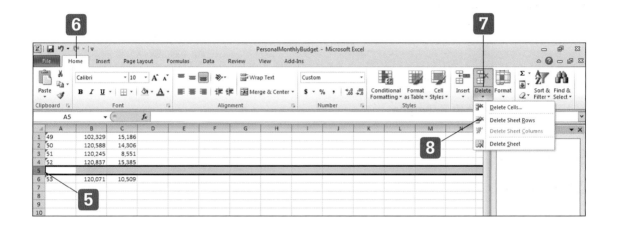

Hide or display a worksheet

Worksheets are easily accessible in a workbook, but you may not want them to be so open. You can hide worksheets so they aren't immediately visible, and then display them again only when you need to work on them. When you hide a worksheet, data in that worksheet can still be used and referenced in formulas and functions in other worksheets.

1 Click the sheet you want to hide.

2 Click the Home tab.

3 Click the Format button.

4 Select Hide & Unhide.

5 Select Hide Sheet from the drop-down list.

6 If a sheet or multiple sheets have been hidden, then the Unhide Sheet option becomes available. Click Unhide Sheet from the drop-down list, select the sheet to be displayed and then click OK.

? DID YOU KNOW?

Hiding one or more worksheets in a workbook does not affect data or formulas in other worksheets; any cell references remain the same.

! ALERT: Hidden worksheets do not appear when you print out a workbook. If you want to print a worksheet that has been hidden, you need to display it first.

Hide or display a workbook

You might want to hide an entire workbook if it contains information you don't want others to see. The command is different from that used to hide an individual worksheet.

1 Open the workbook you want to hide.

2 Click the View tab.

3 Click the Hide button.

4 If the workbook has already been hidden, you won't see it. To unhide it, click the View tab in any open Excel window.

5 Click the Unhide button.

6 From the Unhide dialogue box, select the workbook you want to unhide.

7 Click OK.

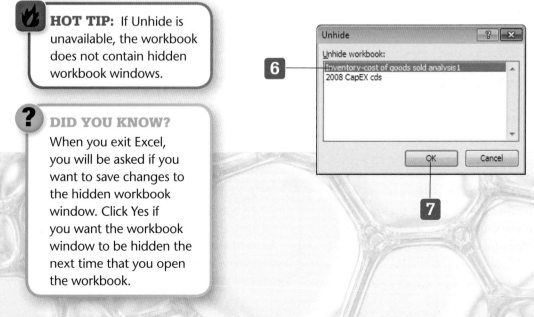

HOT TIP: If Unhide is unavailable, the workbook does not contain hidden workbook windows.

? DID YOU KNOW?

When you exit Excel, you will be asked if you want to save changes to the hidden workbook window. Click Yes if you want the workbook window to be hidden the next time that you open the workbook.

Hide or display a column or row

Before you delete a column or row, consider hiding it instead. By hiding it, you don't cut the information completely. You just make it invisible while you show it to others or print it out. It's easy to display the column or row once again when needed.

1 Select the column or row headers you want to hide.

2 Click the Home tab.

3 Click Format.

4 Click on Hide & Unhide.

5 Select Hide Columns or Hide Rows from the drop-down list.

6 If the columns or rows are hidden, select Unhide Columns or Unhide Rows.

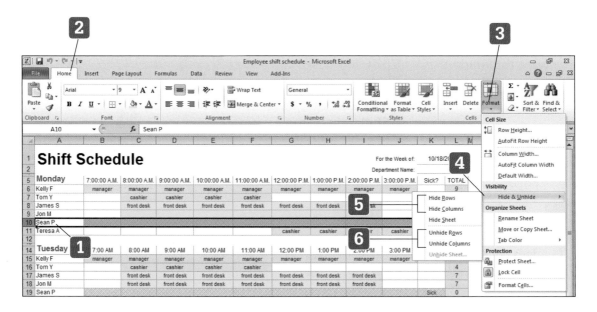

HOT TIP: Drag the mouse pointer to select more than one column or row.

? DID YOU KNOW?

When you hide a column or row, calculations in a worksheet are not affected. All formulas still reference the hidden data if necessary.

Freeze or unfreeze a column or row

Worksheets can quickly become so full of information that, when you scroll to the bottom of the sheet, you can no longer see the top of the sheet. Instead of having to scroll up or down, you can temporarily freeze a column or row so it stays in place on screen no matter where you scroll in the file.

1 Select the column to the right of the column you want to freeze and select the row below the row(s) you want to freeze.

2 Click the View tab.

3 Click the Freeze Panes button, and then select the option you want from the drop-down list:

- Freeze Panes keeps rows and columns visible and in place.

- Freeze Top Row freezes the top row.

- Freeze First Column freezes the first column.

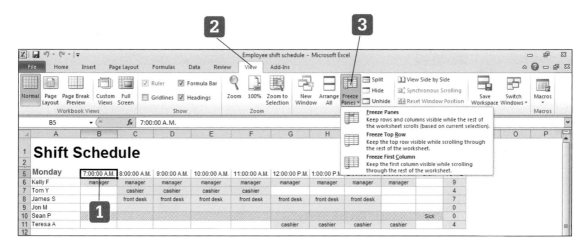

? DID YOU KNOW?

You can split a screen into up to four panes and freeze two of the panes.

? DID YOU KNOW?

You can edit data in a frozen pane as you would another pane, but the cells in the pane still remain stationary.

Adjust column width or row height

What happens if you add long strings of data or larger font sizes? If some of your data or labels disappear, you can adjust each column width to fit its contents and you can also adjust your row heights.

1 Select the column or row header you want to adjust. You can select more columns or rows by dragging.

2 Click the Home tab.

3 Click the Format button.

4 Select Column Width or Row Height from the drop-down list.

5 Type a new column width or row height in points

6 Click OK.

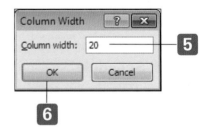

? DID YOU KNOW?

If you use AutoFit, columns or rows will be resized to the width or height of their largest entry.

? DID YOU KNOW?

There are 72 points in one inch. That's a measurement that's used to size text and space on a worksheet.

? DID YOU KNOW?

To change the default column width, click the Home tab, click the Format button, click Default Width, type a column width in points and then click OK.

Divide a worksheet into panes

If you are working with a worksheet that contains many computer screens' worth of data, you can't see the entire contents at once. Rather than having to scroll up and down between different parts of the file, you can divide it into four panes. That way you can scroll independently through each of the two parts of the worksheet and work with both parts at once.

1 Click a cell, column or row to select the area of the file where you want to create separate panes.

2 Click the View tab.

3 Click the Split button.

4 If you want to remove the split and return to one pane, click the Split button again.

? DID YOU KNOW?

If you select a cell, you split the worksheet into four panes. If you select a row or column, you divide it in two.

? DID YOU KNOW?

Once you have two panes, you can resize them by dragging the drag bar at the bottom right-hand corner of the Excel window or by clicking and dragging the pane divider up and down.

Format numbers

Numeric formats can be applied to numbers to better reflect the type of information they represent. That way the appearance of the data in the cells of a worksheet can be changed without changing the actual values in the cells.

1 Find the number(s) you want to format and select the cell or range they are in.

2 Click the Home tab.

3 Click the Number Format list arrow.

4 Select a format from the drop-down list.

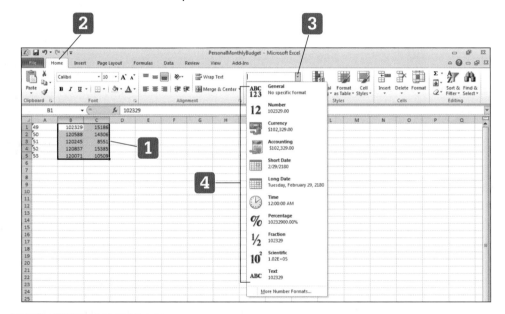

? **DID YOU KNOW?**
You can apply more than one attribute to the range.

? **DID YOU KNOW?**
Numbers can be formatted in international currencies: in the Format Cells dialogue box, click the Number tab, click Currency in the Category list, click the Symbol list arrow, and then click an international currency symbol.

? **DID YOU KNOW?**
The buttons on the Home tab ribbon and mini-toolbar can be simply clicked to turn them on and off.

Format text

By default, 10-point Arial is provided on your computer. But you can change not only the font and its size but also choose different attributes. You should also make sure you're using printer fonts (instead of True Type fonts) if your worksheet will be created for publication.

1 Select the text you want to format.

2 Click the Home tab.

3 To change fonts, click the Font list arrow on the ribbon or mini-toolbar and select the font you want.

4 To change font size, click one or more of the font size buttons on the ribbon or mini-toolbar. Either click the Font Size list arrow, and then click the font size you want, or click the Increase Font Size button or Decrease Font Size Button.

5 To apply other formatting, click one or more of the formatting buttons on the ribbon or mini-toolbar: Bold, Italic, Underline, Shadow, Strikethrough or Font Color.

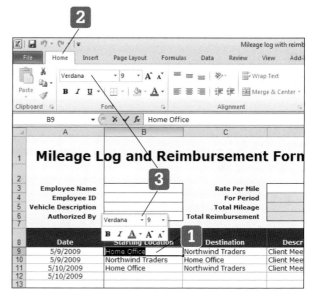

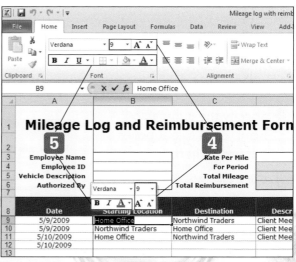

HOT TIP: If you don't want Excel to display the mini-toolbar, you can turn it off in the Excel Options window.

Apply conditional formatting by comparison

Conditional formatting lets the value of a cell determine its formatting. You can use a formula to determine which cells to format or quickly format only top- or bottom-ranked values, values above or below average, or unique or duplicate values.

1 Select the cell or range you want to conditionally format.

2 Click the Home tab.

3 Click the Conditional Formatting button.

4 Select Highlight Cells Rules from the drop-down list.

5 Click the comparison rule you want to apply to conditionally format selected data.

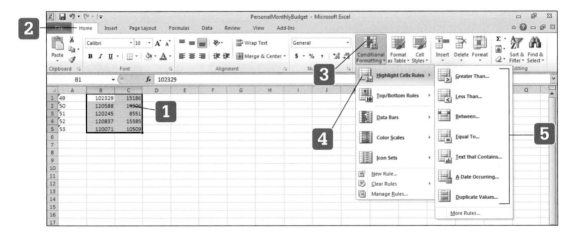

6 Specify the criteria you want. Each rule supplies different criteria.

7 Click OK.

DID YOU KNOW?

When you create a conditional format, you can reference only other cells on the same worksheet or, in certain cases, cells on worksheets in the same currently open workbook. You cannot use conditional formatting on external references to another workbook.

Apply conditional formatting based on ranking and average

This is another type of conditional formatting based on top or bottom ranking, or values that are above or below an average you specify.

1 Select the cell or range you want to conditionally format.

2 Click the Home tab.

3 Click the Conditional Formatting button.

4 Select Top/Bottom Rules from the drop-down list.

5 Select the comparison rule you want to apply to conditionally format selected data.

6 Specify the criteria you want. Each rule supplies different criteria.

7 Click OK.

? DID YOU KNOW?

Conditional formatting can make your spreadsheets more useful if used appropriately. Conditional formatting allows Excel to apply a defined format to cells that meet specific criteria. These formats might include a different background colour, font colour or border. The goal is to make important cells stand out so you can find them more easily.

Manage conditional formatting

When you apply conditional formatting to a cell or range of cells, Excel stores the rules associated with the conditional formatting in the Conditional Formatting Rules Manager. You can use the Conditional Formatting Rules Manager to create, edit, delete and view all conditional formatting rules in a workbook. When two or more conditional formatting rules apply to the same cells, the rules are evaluated in order of precedence as they appear in the dialogue box. You can move a rule up or down in the precedence list. Conditional formatting takes precedence over a manual format, which doesn't appear in the Conditional Formatting Rules Manager.

1 Select the cell or range with the conditional formatting rules you want to edit.

2 Click the Home tab.

3 Click the Conditional Formatting button.

4 Select Manage Rules from the drop-down list.

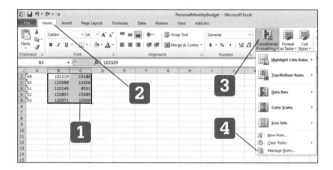

5 Click the Show formatting rulers for list arrow, and then select an option to show the rules you want.

6 Specify the rule you want to change:

- To create a new rule, click New Rule and follow the instructions in the wizard.

- To delete a rule, click Delete Rule.

- To edit a rule, click Edit Rule, make the changes you want and then click OK.

- To move the selected rule up or down in precedence, click the Move Up or Move Down arrow, respectively.

- To stop rule evaluation at a specific rule, select the Stop If True check box.

7 Click OK.

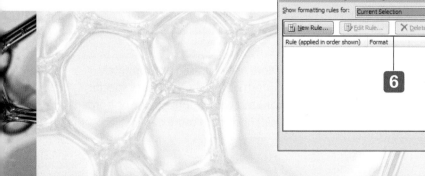

Add colour to cells

Fill colours and can make your data stand out and can lend consistency to related information in a worksheet. When you no longer need cell formatting, you can remove it.

1 To apply a solid colour to a cell, begin by selecting the cell or range you want to format.

2 Click the Home tab.

3 Click the Fill Color button arrow.

4 Select a colour from the palette.

5 To remove the cell shading, select the No Fill option.

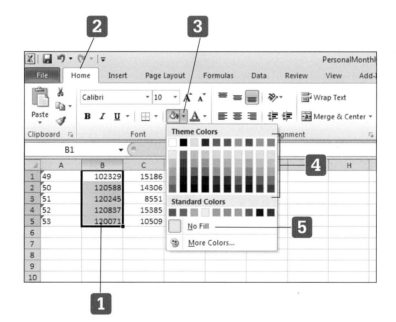

HOT TIP: You can also apply a colour to a cell or group of cells by right-clicking on the cells, selecting Format Cells from the context menu, clicking the Fill tab and selecting a colour from the palette.

Apply a pattern to a cell

Shading gives you another option for calling attention to cells. Shading is especially useful when a worksheet already contains a lot of colours and you want data to stand out even more.

1 Select the cell you want to format.

2 Click the Home tab.

3 Click the Font dialogue box launcher.

4 Click the Fill tab.

5 Click the Pattern Color list arrow, and then click a pattern color.

6 Click the Pattern Style list arrow, and then click a pattern.

7 Click OK.

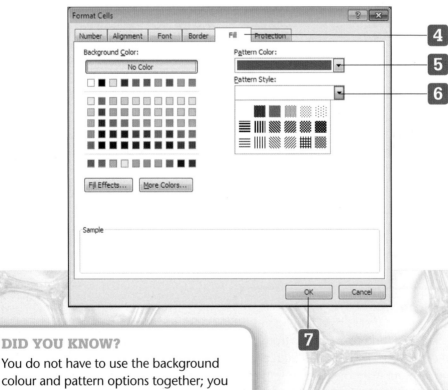

? **DID YOU KNOW?**

You do not have to use the background colour and pattern options together; you can use just a pattern or just a colour.

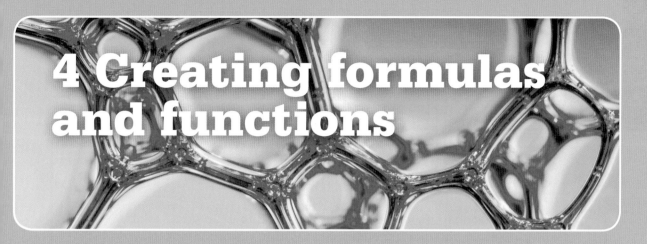

4 Creating formulas and functions

Introduction

In the previous chapter, you learned how to modify your workbook by adding, deleting and moving worksheets within the workbook. Now you're ready to work with commands and references that calculate values and procedures that produce a result. The result can be a sum, an average or a wide variety of more specific options. In order to create formulas, you can use constants (such as the number 101), operators such as the plus or minus sign, functions that specify what action to perform, and references to cells in your worksheet.

Some Excel features help you do your work more efficiently by avoiding trouble. Formula AutoCorrect is an example: when you press the equals sign (=), Formula AutoCorrect is automatically activated. As you type your formula, valid (and correctly spelled) commands appear in a convenient drop-down list. This chapter describes basic operations you can perform with Excel simply and easily.

Formulas in Excel can be as simple or complex as you need. Excel automatically recalculates formulas as you continue to work on a file, so your worksheets remain accurate and up-to-date at all times. You can always make changes to formulas in order to revise the data your worksheet contains.

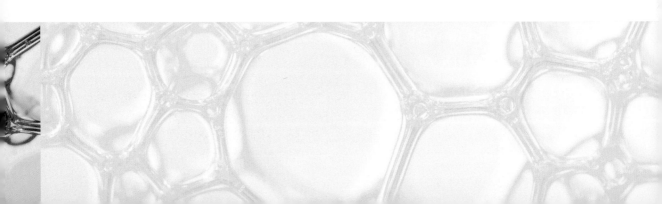

Create a basic formula

Formulas are powerful features of Excel worksheets. They calculate values you have entered and return results for you. Excel provides you with a set of operators that you can use to perform addition, multiplication, division and other calculations. Each formula starts with an argument: the cell references or values that combine to produce a result. If your formula gets too long, you can resize the formula bar to accommodate it.

1 Click the cell that you want to contain the formula.

2 Type the equals sign (=) so Excel can calculate the values you enter. (If you don't, Excel will simply display what you type.)

3 Enter the first argument – a number or a cell reference.

4 Enter an operator such as the plus (+) for addition or asterisk (*) for multiplication.

5 Enter the next argument and repeat values and operators as needed.

6 Press Enter or click the Enter button (the tick) on the formula bar. The result appears in the cell.

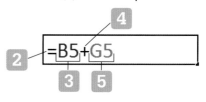

HOT TIP: Point to a cell rather than typing its address so you reduce the chance of typing errors.

? **DID YOU KNOW?**
By default, only formula results are displayed in a cell, but you can adjust the worksheet view to display the formula itself.

Display formulas

By default, formulas aren't displayed in your worksheet cells. When you press Enter or click the Enter button on the formula bar, the calculation you have specified is performed. You may want to display formulas in the cells rather than automatically calculating them, however. Do so by following these steps:

1 Click the Formulas tab.

2 Click Show Formulas.

3 Click the Show Formulas button again to disable the formula display.

HOT TIP: Press Ctrl+ (Ctrl and the + key) to choose Show Formulas.

Activate Formula AutoComplete

One of Excel 2007's most useful new features is Formula AutoComplete. It provides you with suggestions of valid functions, arguments, defined names and other items that help you accurately complete a formula without typing everything from scratch. In order to use this feature, you first have to activate it.

1 Click the File tab.

2 Click Options.

3 Click Formulas.

4 Select the Formula AutoComplete check box.

5 Click OK.

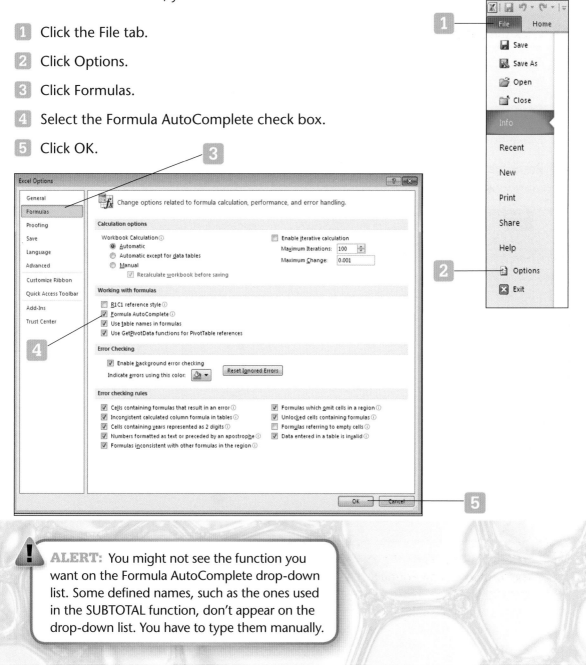

ALERT: You might not see the function you want on the Formula AutoComplete drop-down list. Some defined names, such as the ones used in the SUBTOTAL function, don't appear on the drop-down list. You have to type them manually.

Use Formula AutoComplete

Once you activate Formula AutoComplete, the feature starts working automatically the moment you type the equals sign (=) to begin a formula. After the equals sign, when you type a text string, a drop-down list appears with items that will help you complete your typing.

1 Click the cell where you want to enter the formula.

2 Type = (the equals sign and some beginning letters of a formula) to start Formula AutoComplete.

3 Scan the list of valid items, which changes as you type.

4 Make note of the tool tip that explains what the formula or other item does.

5 Press Tab or double-click an item to select it.

? **DID YOU KNOW?**

The text just before the cursor determines what appears in the Formula AutoComplete drop-down list.

? **DID YOU KNOW?**

After you insert the function, argument, defined name or other element from the Formula AutoComplete list, you need to type function-specific arguments, such as numeric or text values or cell references, to complete the function.

Edit a formula

It's not difficult to edit a formula, especially since the formula bar just above your worksheet data is available for this purpose. But there are a couple of tricks you need to perform in order to enter edit mode and make necessary changes.

1 Select the cell that contains the formula you need to edit.

2 Press F2 to enter Edit mode.

3 Use the Home, End and arrow keys to move through the formula so you can make edits.

4 Press Backspace or Del (Delete) to remove items so you can make corrections.

5 When you're done, click Enter on the formula bar (the tick) or press Enter.

> **HOT TIP:** You can also edit formulas using the copy, cut and paste operations, as you would any other content.

Copy a formula

If you need to copy a formula from one location to another, you have two options: you can use the Clipboard, or use the AutoFill feature. Since the Clipboard option is relatively simple (select the cell, click Copy, click the destination cell and then click Paste), these steps focus on AutoFill.

1 Select the cell that contains the formula you want to copy.

2 Position the mouse pointer over the fill handle at the lower right-hand corner of the cell you just selected.

3 Drag the mouse down until you have selected all of the cells where you want to paste the formula, and then release the mouse button.

? DID YOU KNOW?

You can use the Paste Special command to copy only formulas and not the data contained in the cell. Select the cells that contain the formulas you want to copy, click Copy, click where you want to paste, click Paste Special, click Formulas and click OK.

HOT TIP: If you need to recalculate formulas, press the F9 key.

Use absolute cell references

Sometimes, you'll want a formula to perform an action on a specific cell, even if you copy or move the formula to another worksheet. You can do so by creating an absolute cell reference.

1 Click the cell where you want to enter the formula.

2 Type the equals sign (=) to begin the formula.

3 Select a cell, and then type an operator (+, –, * or /).

4 Select another cell and press the F4 key to make the reference to that cell absolute.

5 When you are done, press Enter or click the Enter button (the tick) on the formula bar.

Use mixed cell references

You have the option of creating not only formulas that contain absolute or relative cell references but also mixed references. A mixed reference is either an absolute column and relative row or an absolute row and relative column. When you add the $ symbol before the column letter or the row number you make the reference absolute.

1 Click the cell that you want to contain the formula.

2 Type the equals sign (=).

3 Select the cell you want to refer to and complete the formula.

4 Click to position the cursor in the formula bar and type $ before the column or row you want to make absolute. For example, A$1 is relative for column A and absolute for row 1, while $A1 is absolute for column A and relative for row 1.

5 Click the Enter button on the formula bar (the tick) or press Enter.

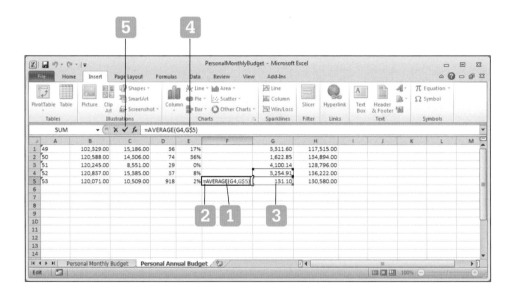

Name a cell or range with the Name box

Rather than making a reference to a range of cells, you can name those cells. Treating them as a single entity with a name makes them easier to remember. It's also easier to type a name such a 'customers' in a formula rather than a range such as (B10:B105).

1 Select the cell or range of cells you want to name.

2 Click the Name box at the left edge of the formula bar.

3 Type a name of up to 255 characters for the range and press Enter.

Identify a cell or range with the New Name dialogue box

You can also designate a name for a cell or range with the New Name dialogue box. This option requires a few more steps than in the preceding task. But you gain more control over the naming process, and you can name a workbook or worksheet as well.

1 Select the cell or range you want to name.

2 Click the Formulas tab.

3 Click Define Name.

4 Type a name for the cell or range.

5 Select a scope for the name, for instance the workbook or a tab.

6 Click OK.

Add a named cell or range to a formula

Once you define a name for a cell or range, you can add it to a formula in one of several ways. You can use the Name box, take advantage of Formula AutoComplete, or use the Use in Formula command.

1 Click the Name box down arrow.

2 Select the name you want from the list. The selected name appears in the Name box and all cells referenced by the name are selected.

3 To use Formula AutoComplete, type the equals sign (=) to start a formula.

4 Type the first letter of the name you want to use.

5 Select the name from the drop-down list, and press Tab or double-click the name to add it to the formula.

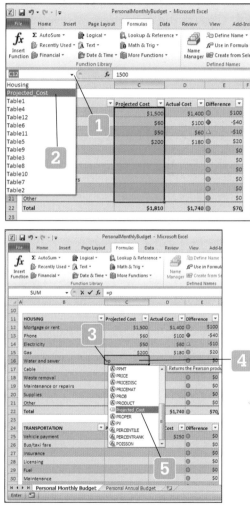

HOT TIP: By default, names use absolute rather than relative cell references.

? DID YOU KNOW?

A name can include uppercase or lowercase letters; names are not case sensitive.

Enter a name with the Use in Formula command

The Use in Formula command comes in handy when you have a set of names you have already created and you need to choose between them.

1 Click in the cell where you want to add the formula.

2 Type the equals sign (=).

3 Click the Formulas tab.

4 Click the Use in Formula button.

5 Select one of the available menu options:

- Click the name you want to use in the formula.

- Click Paste Names, select a name and click OK.

? DID YOU KNOW?

Once you adopt the practice of using names in your workbook, you can easily update, audit and manage these names.

Organise names

Once you have added a group of names to a document, you'll need to delete or work with them. The Name Manager dialogue box lists all of your defined names and table names in one location.

1 Click the Formulas tab.

2 Click the Name Manager button.

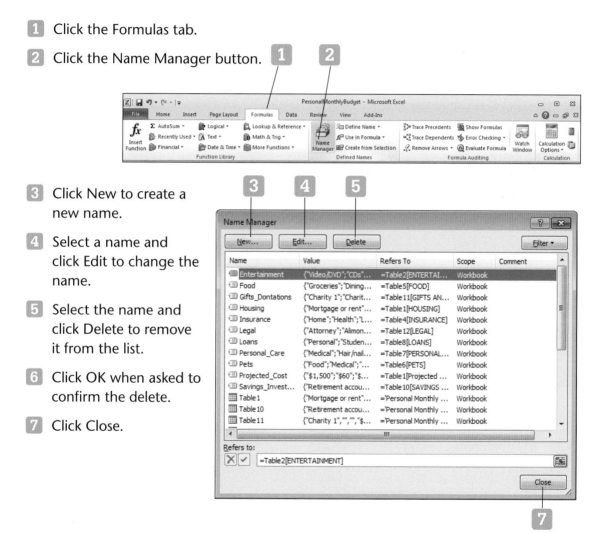

3 Click New to create a new name.

4 Select a name and click Edit to change the name.

5 Select the name and click Delete to remove it from the list.

6 Click OK when asked to confirm the delete.

7 Click Close.

ALERT: The Name Manager will not appear while you are editing a cell.

Simplify a formula with ranges

Formulas can become complicated, and the more complex they are, the greater the possibility of errors. One way to simplify a formula is to use ranges or names. The preceding several tasks have examined creating and adding names to formulas. When you want to add a range of cells in a formula, follow these quick steps:

1 Click the cell where you would like the formula to be contained.

2 Click the equals sign (=) and a function to begin the formula.

3 Click the first cell of the range.

4 Drag to the last cell in the range. The range address is automatically added to the formula.

5 Type the closing parenthesis to complete the formula.

6 Press Enter or click the Enter button (the tick) on the formula bar.

HOT TIP: If you need to add a name as well as a range, press F3 and choose the name from the list that appears.

Display calculations with the status bar

Sometimes, a formula isn't the easiest way to accomplish a task with Excel. For instance, if you need to perform a calculation just to get a preview of a result, you can do so with the status bar. It can display the sum, average, maximum minimum or count of selected values.

1 Select the cell or range you want to calculate. The sum, average and count of the selected cells appear immediately on the status bar.

2 If you need to see the maximum, minimum or other result, right-click the status bar.

3 Click an option in the context menu to toggle it on or off.

? DID YOU KNOW?

When you use the status bar for a calculation, you don't see the results in the worksheet when they are printed.

? DID YOU KNOW?

Cells that contain text are not part of status bar calculations, unless you use the Count function.

Calculate totals with AutoSum

Another option for quickly adding up a group of cells is the AutoSum button on Excel's standard toolbar. The advantage of using AutoSum over the status bar is that AutoSum suggests the range to sum. You can change the range if necessary.

1 Click the cell where you want the calculation to be displayed.

- To add up a range of number, select the range of cells.

- To add up only some of the numbers in a range, select each cell using the Ctrl key.

- To add up a table of numbers, select the cells and leave an additional column to the right and a row at the bottom.

2 Click the Formulas tab.

3 Click the AutoSum button.

4 Press Enter or click the Enter button (the tick) on the formula bar.

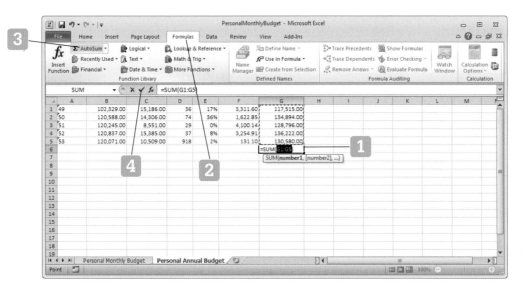

Convert formulas to values

If you have cells in a worksheet that contain formulas, you can easily convert the cells to values only. You might want to do this if you want the cells to remain constant. One quick option is to use the Paste Special command to paste the contents of the range into the cell to replace the formula.

1 Select the range of cells with formulas that you want to convert to values.

2 Click the Home tab.

3 Click the Copy button.

4 Click the Paste button.

5 Select Paste Special from the drop-down list.

6 Select the Values option.

7 Click OK, then press Esc to leave Copy mode.

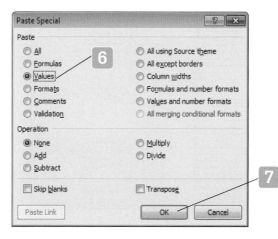

? DID YOU KNOW?

You can delete values and keep formulas in a cell. Click the Find & Select button on the Home tab, click Go To Special, click the Constants option, click the Numbers check box, and clear the other check boxes under Formula. Then click OK. Press Delete to remove the values.

Create a custom calculation

Custom formulas perform calculations let you really get to the heart of your data by analysing it in relation to itself. What this means is that you can do sophisticated analysis to draw out less obvious information from your data. With the new information in hand, you can then present it in a clear and easily understood way with a PivotTable report.

1 Modify your PivotTable in the PivotTable Field List. In this example, the Housing, Projected Cost, Actual Cost and Difference fields have been selected.

2 Right-click anywhere within the PivotTable data, and select Value Field Settings from the resulting context menu.

3 Click the Show Values As tab.

4 Select Running Total In from the Show values as drop-down list. Note: You cannot select something presented in your report as a sum of values, only something listed as a row or column label. On second thought, you can, but your settings will produce a meaningless table populated by pound signs.

5 Select Projected Costs as your Base field, so that the resulting report will show how many units each employee sold, and display only how much revenue was generated.

6 Click OK. As you can see, profits are now only listed for the Units rows, clearing up the report and making it easier to read.

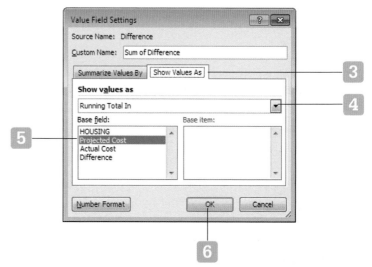

The types of custom calculations you can perform on your PivotTable data are listed in Table 4.1.

Table 4.1 Custom calculations

Calculation	What it does
Normal	Summarises the Values area field
Difference From	Uses the difference between a base and field item to summarise data
% Of	Uses the percentage of a base field item to summarise data
% Difference From	Uses the percentage of difference between a base and field item to summarize data
Running Total In	Shows data as a running total in a base field
% Of Row	Uses the percentage of total row value to display data
% Of Column	Uses the percentage of total column value to display data
% Total	Uses percentage of the total value from the report to display data
Index	Uses the formula: ((Cell Value)*(Grand Total of Grand Totals))/((Grand Row Total)*(Grand Column Total))

? DID YOU KNOW?

You can create a slicer in an existing PivotTable or create a standalone slicer. A slicer can also be shared by connecting to another PivotTable.

5 Working with charts

Introduction

In the previous chapter, you learned how to work with commands and references that calculate values, and procedures that produce a result. Now you're ready to create and modify charts. For many people, a page full of numbers arranged in cells is not the easiest way to absorb and understand data. Visual representations are far more effective at presenting an overview than numbers alone, even if numbers are effectively formatted. A chart gives users a snapshot of trends and patterns that can facilitate decision making.

Excel gives you a variety of presentation formats for charts. The option you select can be tailored to the type of data you want to present. You can turn your numbers into a bar, line, pie, surface or bubble chart to help your colleagues reach conclusions about the data you have gathered.

This chapter will examine how to create and tailor charts that illustrate trends as well as interconnections between numbers. One set of data can be related to another, and a chart can demonstrate this at a glance. You'll also learn how to change a chart type as needed, how to display data in a different style, or how to move or resize your chart to optimise the information you want to present.

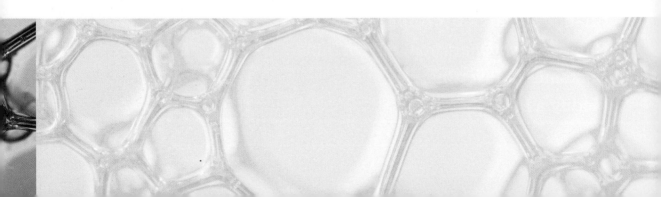

Select the type of chart you need

Excel gives you plenty of options when it comes to creating the right type of chart for your needs. Your job is to select the chart that presents data in just the right way. If you want to compare parts of a whole, select a pie chart. To compare different figures across geographic regions, select a column chart. When you need to track data as it changes through time, select an area chart.

1 Select the data you want to present in the form of a chart.

2 Click the Insert tab.

3 Click one of the common chart types in the Charts tool group.

4 Select a sub-type from the type of chart you selected.

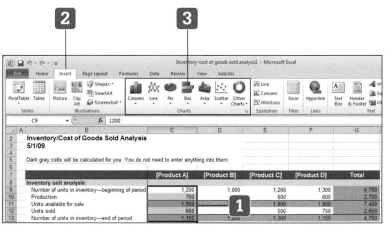

? DID YOU KNOW?

Charts in Excel have a set of essential elements: title – text that identifies the purpose of a chart; data marker – a bar, circle, dot or other object that illustrates a data point; y-axis – the vertical axis of a chart; x-axis – the horizontal axis of a chart; data series – a set of related data points in a chart; legend – instructions that explain the colours or symbols in a chart.

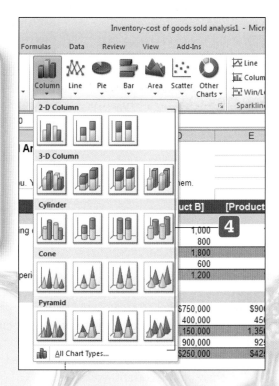

Select from all chart types

The previous task outlined the general steps involved in creating a chart with Excel. As you can see, it's a quick process. You can either create an embedded chart – a chart that is embedded in an existing worksheet – or one that is displayed on its own worksheet. If you open the Charts dialogue box launcher, you can select from among all the available chart types.

1 Select the data you want to present in the chart.

2 Click the Insert tab.

3 Click the Charts dialogue box launcher.

4 Click a chart category.

5 Select an option.

6 Click OK.

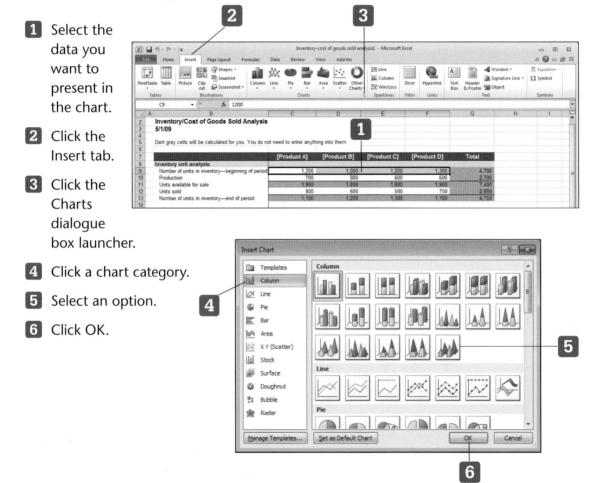

HOT TIP: To create a default chart, select the data you want to present, then press F11 to create the chart on a new sheet, or Alt+F1 to create an embedded chart on the current worksheet.

? DID YOU KNOW?
Embedding a chart in an existing worksheet is a good option when you want to view chart data separately from worksheet data.

Select parts of a chart

In order to edit or work with a chart once you create it, you need to select its elements. A chart element is an object that makes up the chart – an axis, the legend or the data series.

1 Click anywhere in the chart to select it. The Chart Tools tabs appear above the ribbon.

2 Click either the Format or Layout tab.

3 Click the down arrow next to Chart Elements.

4 Click the chart element you want to select. When you have selected a chart element, selection handles appear around it.

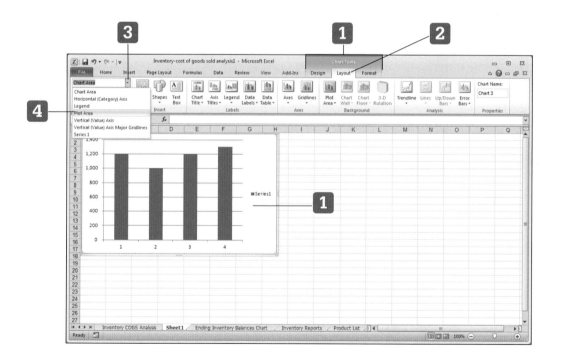

HOT TIP: Click a chart element directly within the chart to select it quickly.

SEE ALSO: The parts of a chart are listed at the start of this chapter, in 'Select the type of chart you need'.

Edit a chart

You can edit a chart by changing any of its features at any time. You might want to change the colours associated with a bar, line or other element, for instance. When you edit a chart, you do not change the data used to create it. You only change the presentation.

1 Select the part of the chart you want to edit.

2 Click the Design tab to change colours or change other visual elements.

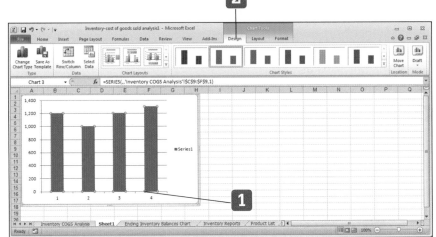

3 Click the Layout tab to change any part of the chart.

4 Click a button available and select an option from the drop-down list.

? DID YOU KNOW?

If you want to edit the data range, you can select the data series on the worksheet, and drag the outline to include more or less data in the chart.

🔥 HOT TIP: Point to any object in a chart to see what it's called.

Format chart elements

The Format tab, which appears under Chart Tools when you select a chart, contains options that control the way data is presented. The formatting options differ depending on the element you have selected.

1 Click anywhere in the chart to select it.

2 Click the Format tab.

3 Click the Format Selection button.

4 Select the options you want. The precise options differ, but those for Border Styles include:

- Width: This adjusts border thickness, in points.

- Compound type: If the border style is compound (i.e. it contains two styles), the combination appears here.

- Dash type: If the border is a dash, the type appears here.

- Cap type: If the border includes a cap, select whether it should be square, round or flat.

- Join type: Determines whether the join between top and side is bevelled, round or flat.

- Arrow settings: Determines the style of an arrow's two ends.

5 Click Close.

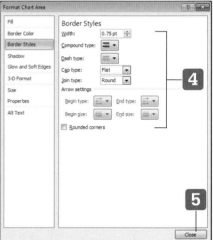

HOT TIP: Instead of using the ribbon commands, you can also right-click a chart element and then select the chart element from the context menu.

Move a chart

If you are working with a chart that has been embedded in a worksheet, you can move it easily. That way it won't interfere with the other data on the sheet.

1 Click anywhere in the chart you want to move to select it.

2 Position the mouse pointer over a blank area of the chart, then click and drag the pointer. The outline of the chart moves to indicate that it is being moved to a new location.

3 Release the mouse button.

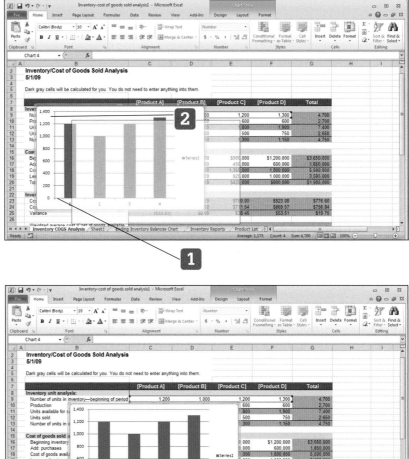

? DID YOU KNOW?

If you have created a chart in a new worksheet rather than embedding it in a worksheet that has existing content, the position and size of the chart are fixed, and determined by the chart's contents.

Resize a chart

When you click on a chart element such as its legend, selection handles appear around that element. When you click in an empty part of a chart, selection handles appear at the corners and the sides of the chart. Click and drag any of the chart selection handles to resize the chart.

1 Click an empty area of the chart you want to resize to select it.

2 Position the mouse pointer over one of the selection handles.

3 Drag the handle to resize it and then release the mouse button.

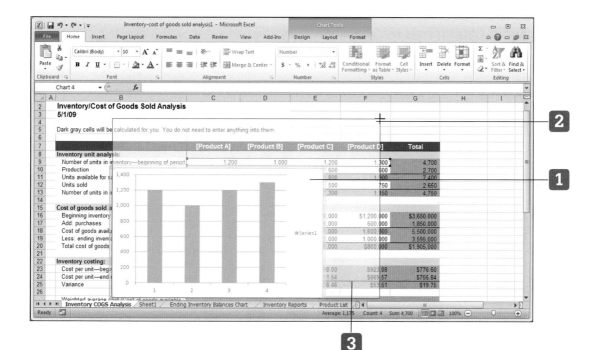

ALERT: If you resize a chart by dragging it downward, make sure you don't interfere with legends or axis titles.

HOT TIP: If you want to restore the chart to its previous size, press Ctrl+Z to undo the resizing.

Edit a chart's title

When you create a chart, it typically includes a title, axis titles and a legend. You can adjust the position and contents of the title if the data changes or if you want to emphasise part of the contents.

1 Click anywhere in the chart you want to edit. The Chart Tools tab appears.

2 Click the Layout tab.

3 Click the Chart Title button, and select one of the options that appear:

- None will make the title invisible.

- Centered Overlay Title adds a title without resizing the chart to accommodate it.

- Above Chart moves the chart title to the top and resizes the chart.

- More Title Options lets you specify custom chart title settings.

4 Double-click the title text box to position the cursor, and change the title if needed.

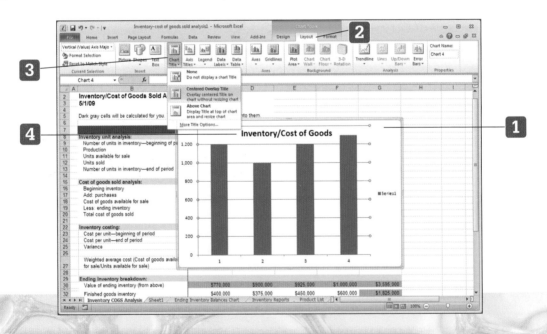

? DID YOU KNOW?

A title that is formatted as an overlay does not overlap other chart contents; the chart is resized so the title does not interfere with it. A title that is formatted as an overlap has its text on top of the chart, so the text might appear to be on top of bars, axes or other contents.

Change chart labels

You can change the legend and data labels in your chart at any time. The legend is text that helps viewers understand colours and symbols used in the chart with the data they represent. Data labels are values next to the bars, lines, dots or other objects that make data easier to interpret.

1 Select the chart you want to edit. The Chart Tools tab appears.

2 Click the Layout tab.

3 Click the Legend button, and then select one of the available options.

4 Click the Data Labels button, and then select one of the Data Labels options to either show or hide the labels.

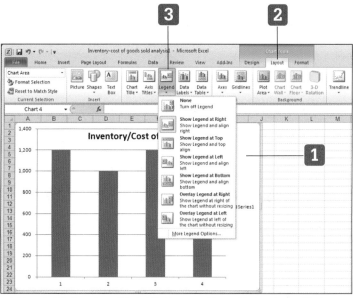

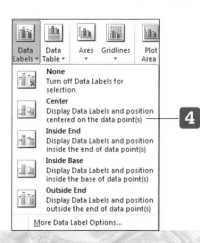

? DID YOU KNOW?

The first two data label options let you show or hide the labels. The third lets you specify custom options: you can select what text they contain, decide on their position, and select a separator to go between them.

? DID YOU KNOW?

The first four table legend options after None control where the legend appears in relation to the chart. The next two overlay options position the legend either on the right or left. The last option, More Legend Options, lets you specify custom options for your legend.

Change a chart's type

If one of your colleagues doesn't understand what your chart is intended to portray, you can try another option for presenting your data. Excel gives you plenty of chart options from which to select, including both 2-D and 3-D layouts.

1 Click anywhere in the chart you want to change to select it. The Chart Tools tab appears.

2 Click the Design tab.

3 Click the Change Chart Type button.

The Change Chart Type dialogue box appears.

4 Select the type of chart you want.

5 Select the specific subtype of chart.

6 Click OK.

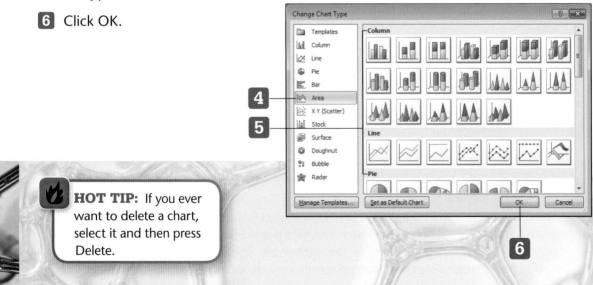

HOT TIP: If you ever want to delete a chart, select it and then press Delete.

Adjust layout and style

Once you select the type of chart you want, you can refine its appearance by adjusting its layout and style. The layout of a chart is the arrangement of elements within its type. For instance, if you select the bar chart type, you can select a 2-D or 3-D layout, or you can decide to have the bars run horizontally rather than vertically. The style of a chart refers to its colour choices as well as its background.

1 Select the chart you want to edit. The Chart Tools tab appears.

2 Click the Design tab.

3 Scroll through the sets of layouts and select the layout you want.

4 In the Chart Styles section under the Design tab, click the scroll up or down arrows and select the style you want.

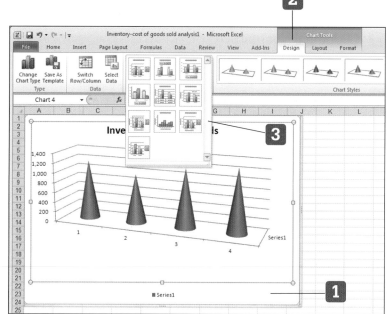

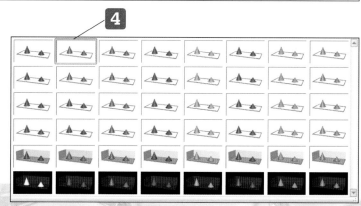

? **DID YOU KNOW?**

You can customise your chart by choosing different colours or line thicknesses. You can then save your customised settings by clicking Save As Template in the Design tab so you can apply the settings to other charts you create.

Change a chart's axis

An axis is a reference line that borders an edge of a chart, either along one side or along the top or bottom. Axes are typically named x (for vertical), y (for horizontal) or z (for 3-D charts). You might want to change the axes of a chart if the axis labels (the labels next to bars or other objects) become too difficult to read because they are too long.

1 Click the chart to select it. The Chart Tools tab appears.

2 Click the Layout tab.

3 Click the Axes button.

4 Select Primary Horizontal Axis or Primary Vertical Axis from the drop-down list.

5 Select one of the available options.

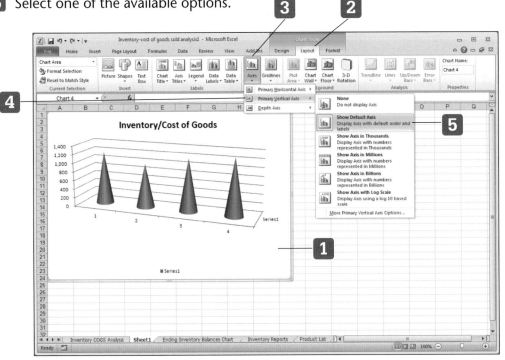

🔥 HOT TIP: If your chart has 3-D objects, click the Axes button, point to Depth Axes and select one of the available formatting commands.

? DID YOU KNOW?

You can also change the gridlines, the lines that run horizontally or vertically behind the chart that help the viewer determine the values of its data points. Click the chart to select it, click the Layout tab, click the Gridlines button and select one of the formatting options.

Work with pie charts

Pie charts are striking and effective tools for presenting parts that make up a whole. You might use a pie chart to illustrate the ethnic groups within a particular population, or the proportions of expenditures within a budget. Excel lets you select predesigned variations on the pie chart theme in order to call attention to individual slices by pulling them out from the adjacent pieces.

1 Select the data you want to format as a pie chart.

2 Click the Insert tab.

3 Click the Pie button and select a simple design from those shown in the drop-down list.

4 Double-click a pie slice to select it.

5 Drag the pie slice out and away from the center to 'explode' it from the pie so it stands out.

6 Release the mouse button.

HOT TIP: You must double-click a pie slice to select it. Single-clicking selects the entire data series, not the slice.

Format chart text

The text that accompanies a chart is formatted in a generic font and style. You may want to format the text to correspond to other documents, or to match your organisation's house style. The text formatting controls on the Home or Format tabs allow you to change the text's appearance.

1 Click the chart to select it.

2 Select the text you want to format.

3 Click the Home tab.

4 Use the text controls to select a font, font size and styles (bold, italic or underline).

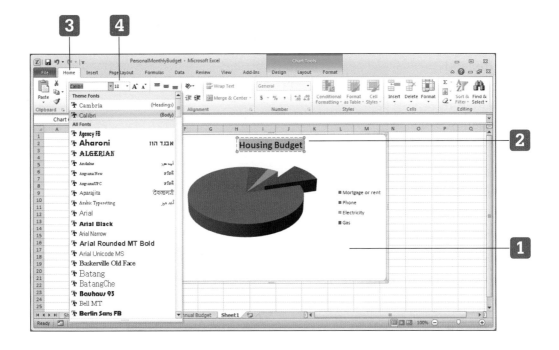

? DID YOU KNOW?

You can highlight all of the text by clicking and dragging across it. You can also select part of the text by clicking to position the insertion point and then pressing Shift+Click at the end of the selection.

? DID YOU KNOW?

You can use WordArt – text that has special effects such as 3-D shapes and shading – to give your chart text more visual interest. Select the text, click the Format tab and select one of the options shown in the WordArt Styles tool group.

Change a chart's background

A chart's readability can be affected by its background. If the background is too bright or too similar in colour to the colours in the chart, it can make the chart hard to read. If the background contrasts strongly, it can make the chart easier to view and gives it a more dramatic effect.

1 Select the chart you want to edit.

2 Click the Layout tab.

3 Click the Chart Wall, Chart Floor, or Plot Area button, depending on which part of the layout you want to change.

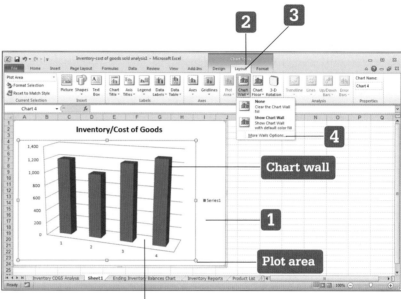

Chart floor

4 Select More Options from the drop-down list.

5 Select the Solid fill option.

6 Click the Color down arrow to open the colour palette.

7 Select a colour from the palette.

8 Click Close.

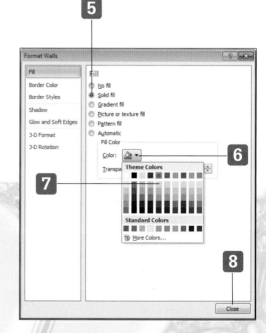

ALERT: 3-D charts use the term chart wall to describe the background, and chart floor to describe the bottom of the chart.

Create a PivotChart from a PivotTable

A PivotTable is part of a worksheet that summarises a list of data using complex and variable criteria. By charting a PivotTable, you give others an overview of the contents and an easy way to draw conclusions because the information is presented visually. When you create a PivotChart, a new tab called Analyze appears. It contains controls for collapsing or expanding fields, refreshing or clearing data, and showing or hiding features such as the Field List.

1 Click anywhere in the PivotTable.

2 Click the Options tab.

3 Click the PivotChart button.

4 Select the layout option you want.

5 Click OK.

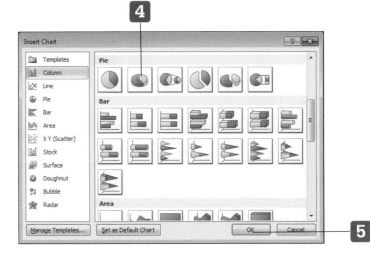

? DID YOU KNOW?

The PivotChart Filter pane lets you filter out data that appears in the chart. Tick the box next to a criterion to add it to the chart; untick it to remove it.

Customise a PivotChart

Even if you create a PivotChart from data presented in a PivotTable, the results aren't 'written in stone'. You can always adjust them to clarify your report. If you ever want to rename a report, just click the Options tab, type the new name in the PivotTable Name box and press Enter.

1 Click the Layout tab to adjust the PivotChart.

2 Click the Format tab to fill shapes, change type designs, or other visual aspects of the chart.

3 Click the Analyze tab to refresh data, clear or add filters, or change the active tab.

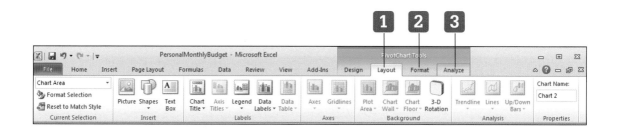

Modify a PivotChart

In Excel 2010, all of the tools available for modifying charts are also available for Pivot Charts. In fact, the PivotChart Tools that appear when you create a Pivot Chart differ from the regular Chart Tools only in that they also include an Analyze tab. Of course, when you create a PivotChart, you have all the flexibility that it provides.

1 Select a substantial amount of data to create your sample Pivot Chart, but not so much that it's hard to create a coherent image.

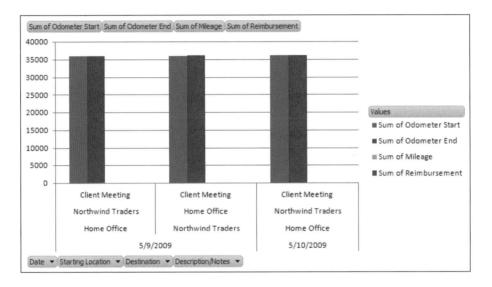

2 Make sure that you've selected only the aforementioned cells to be represented in your Pivot Chart by clicking in the provided range field.

3 Select PivotChart from the Tables group in the Insert tab, and select New Worksheet.

4 Select all of the check boxes in the PivotTable Field List.

5 Click Change Chart Type on the Design tab. Click Column in the Change Chart Type dialogue box.

6 Select the Stacked Column in 3-D option.

7 Click OK.

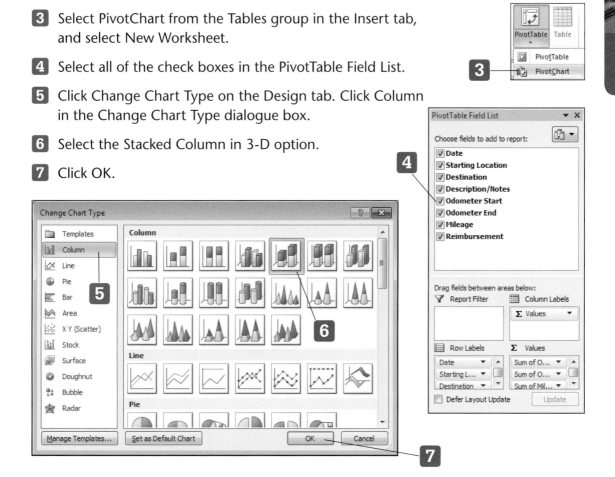

8 Now you can take advantage of all the same customisation options you had with regular charts, but with the added flexibility of a PivotChart.

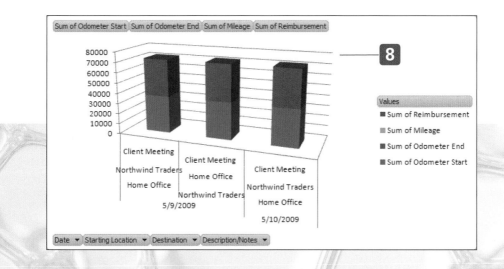

6 Interpreting worksheet data with tables

Introduction

In the previous chapter, you learned how to create and modify charts, including PivotCharts. Now you're ready to analyse and interpret the data in worksheets using tables. Tables (which were known as lists in previous versions) are among one of the most powerful and flexible tools Excel gives you. You can quickly convert a group of cells into a table and use Quick Styles to make its contents easy to interpret.

In order to enter data into tables, you can make use of pick lists, which use rules to restrict what is entered in specified fields. Drop-down lists of entries also enable you to provide consistent data entry for you and your colleagues.

Once your table contains the data you want, you can sort it using buttons on the ribbon, or by making use of the AutoFilter feature. You can also create PivotTables, which highlight data for easier viewing and make it easy for you to add or delete criteria you want to present. Once you learn to work with tables, you'll find they make it easy to present reports or select exactly the information you want your colleagues to analyse so they can make informed decisions.

Create a table

In order to create a table, you first select the data you want to present, as you would any other feature. However, you need to make sure that the field names are positioned in a single row in the first line of the list. In addition, each record in the table should be on a single row. Once you create the table, you can enter data directly in it, in any order; you'll learn to sort the data later in this chapter.

1 Open a blank worksheet.

2 Enter field labels on the first row of the table.

3 Type information for each record in a separate row.

4 Select all the cells in the table, including labels.

5 Do one of the following:

- Click the Table button on the Insert tab.

- Click the Format as Table button on the Home tab, and then select a table style.

6 Adjust the table size, tick the My table has headers box, and click OK.

Table headers

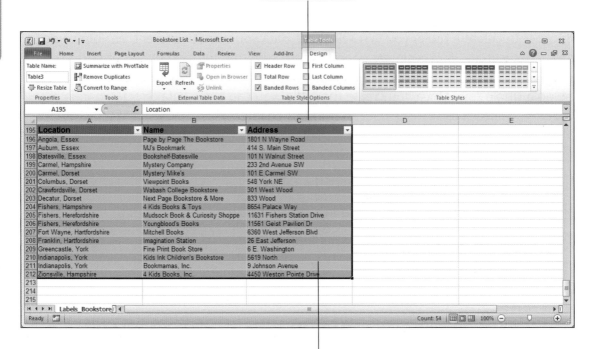

Table data

HOT TIP: To delete a data table, select it and then press Delete to delete the entire table. If you want to keep the cells and just delete the data, click Clear and select Clear Contents.

ALERT: Make sure your table records do not contain any blank rows.

Apply a style to a table

When you click the Format as Table button from the Home tab to create a table, you have the option of formatting the table with predefined formats. However, you can assign colours to the headers and data in a table at any time. You select from a gallery of table styles that is based on the current theme.

2

More button

1 Select a cell, a range of cells or the entire table.

2 Do one of the following:

- Click one of the designs shown in the Table Styles tool group on the Design tab.

1

- Click the Design tab under Table Tools and click the More button, then select a table style from the gallery.

- Click the Home tab, click Format as Table, and select a table style from the gallery.

? DID YOU KNOW?

To clear a table style, click any cell in the table, click the design tab under Table Tools, click the More arrow under Table Styles and click Clear.

? DID YOU KNOW?

If you want to copy a table style from one table to another, use the Format Painter. Select a cell that has the formatting you want to copy, click the Format Painter button on the Home tab, drag to scroll across the cells you want to format, and release the mouse button.

Table Styles gallery

Modify a table style

If you have a design you want to emulate or a set of colours you need to match exactly, you can select a table style and then modify it to suit the needs of the project. You can also create your own custom table style.

1 Click the Home tab.

2 Click the Format as Table button.

3 Select New Table Style to create a new style or you can modify an existing table style.

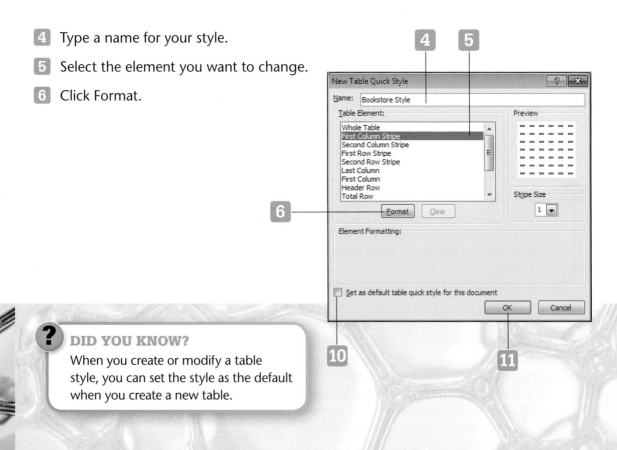

4 Type a name for your style.

5 Select the element you want to change.

6 Click Format.

? **DID YOU KNOW?**

When you create or modify a table style, you can set the style as the default when you create a new table.

7 Click the Font tab to change the font, and the Border tab to select a cell border style.

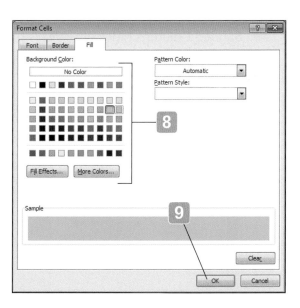

8 Click the Fill tab to select a colour for the table element you have chosen.

9 Select a colour and then click OK.

10 Clear or tick the Set as default table quick style for this document box.

11 Click OK.

? DID YOU KNOW?

You can delete a custom style by clicking the Home tab, clicking the Format as Table button, right-clicking the style you created and choosing Delete.

Show or hide parts of a table

By default, Excel displays a standard set of elements with a table, including headings, columns and rows. You can format the table all at once or any one of these elements individually. You also have the option of hiding formatting elements you no longer need.

1 Select the cell or cell range in the table you want to edit.

2 Under the Table Tools tab, click the Design tab.

3 Clear or tick the box next to the element you want to show or hide:

- Header Row hides or displays the top row of the table.

- Total Row hides or displays a total row at the bottom of the table.

- Banded Rows hides or displays the colour of the rows that have been banded.

- First Column highlights the first column so you can format it.

- Last Column highlights the last column so you can format it

- Banded Columns hides or displays the colour of the columns that have been banded.

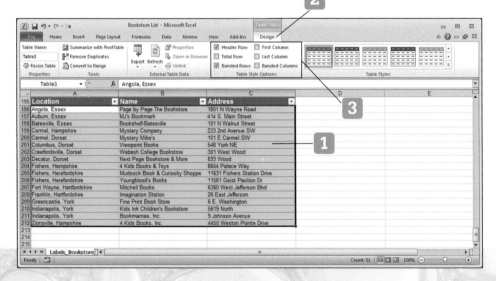

HOT TIP: Ticking an element makes it visible; unticking it hides it.

Total data in a table

One of the best things about data in worksheets is the ability to find totals or perform other calculations quickly. Tables provide you with a Total Row option that instantly finds the total of data in a row

1 Click a cell in a table.

2 Click the Design tab.

3 Select the Total Row check box. A total row is added at the bottom of the table.

4 Click the cell in the column for which you want to calculate a total, and click the drop-down list arrow.

5 Select the calculation you want to perform by choosing it from the drop-down list.

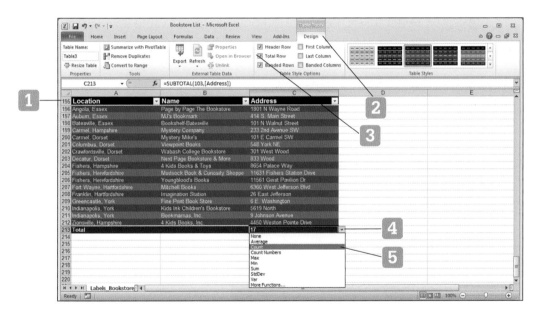

? DID YOU KNOW?

You can calculate data in a column as well by clicking a cell in a blank column and then typing a formula.

? DID YOU KNOW?

When you add a total row at the end of a table, a drop-down list appears for each total cell along with the word Total in the cell at the extreme left. The drop-down list lets you perform a calculation using a function you select.

Insert a row or column

Once you create a table, you can add or delete rows or columns as needed, but the process differs slightly from that for conventional worksheet data. To select column data, click the top edge of the column header. To select an entire column, double-click the top edge of the header. To click a row, click its left border. To select an entire table, double-click the upper left-hand corner.

1 Click a cell in the table, or select a row or column.

2 Click the Home tab.

3 Click the Insert button, and from the drop-down list select one of the following:

- To add a column, select Insert Table Columns to the Left or Insert Table Columns to the Right.

- To add a row, select Insert Table Rows Above or Insert Table Rows Below.

HOT TIP: To select only the data in a table rather than the entire table, single-click the upper left-hand corner and press Ctrl+A.

Resize a table

Often you will need to resize a table, either to make it easier to read or more compact so it fits better next to other contents.

1️⃣ Click anywhere in the table.

2️⃣ Click the Design tab.

3️⃣ Click Resize Table.

4️⃣ Type the range of cells you want the table to fill.

5️⃣ Click OK.

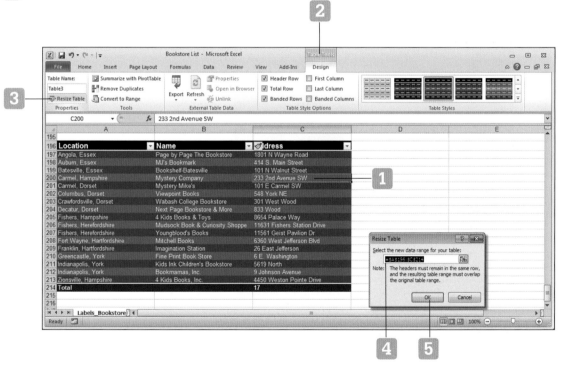

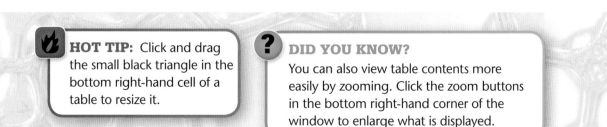

🔥 **HOT TIP:** Click and drag the small black triangle in the bottom right-hand cell of a table to resize it.

❓ **DID YOU KNOW?**
You can also view table contents more easily by zooming. Click the zoom buttons in the bottom right-hand corner of the window to enlarge what is displayed.

Delete rows or columns

It's a good idea to keep tables compact and to delete rows or columns if you no longer need them. You can do so by using a range of Delete options on the Home tab.

1 Click any cell in the row or column you want to remove.

2 Click the Home tab.

3 Click the Delete button, and then select Delete Table Rows or Delete Table Columns from the drop-down list.

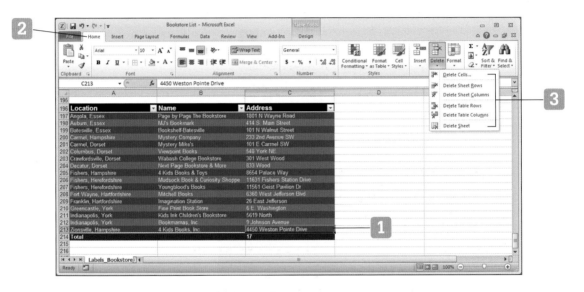

? **DID YOU KNOW?**

Excel can find and remove rows you have accidentally duplicated. Click the Design tab, click Remove Duplicates, select the columns in the row you want to remove (or click Select All to select the entire row) and click OK.

! **ALERT:** The Delete button is different to the Cut button. The Cut button only removes selected contents to the Clipboard. Delete lets you select which table elements to remove; you can only restore them using the Undo command.

Enter data with a drop-down list

Typing data item by item can be time-consuming. A faster way is to enter data from a drop-down list, also called a PickList. The PickList feature becomes available once you have entered at least one record in a list. It makes suggestions based on your previous entries; if you are entering a series of records that include the same city or postal code, for instance, you can select it from a list rather than typing the characters repetitively.

1 Right-click the cell in which you want to enter data chosen from a list.

2 Select Pick from Drop-down List from the context menu.

3 Make a selection from the list.

4 Press Enter or Tab to accept the choice and add it to the cell.

HOT TIP: You can press Esc to cancel the entry if you want to make another choice.

Create a drop-down list

If you don't see the data entry options you want in the drop-down list Excel gives you, you can create your own custom drop-down list. A custom list is useful because it gives you and your colleagues a way to enter data consistently.

1 Type a set of entries in the order you want.

2 Select the range of cells.

3 Click the Name box, type a name, and press Enter.

4 Select the cell where you want the drop-down list to appear.

5 Click the Data tab.

6 Click the Data Validation button.

ALERT: Make sure the cells you want to include in the drop-down list don't include any blank cells.

7 Click the Settings tab.

8 Click the Allow down arrow, and then select List.

9 Enter the values you want.

10 Click the Input Message tab, and type a message to be displayed when someone makes an invalid entry.

11 Click the Error Alert tab, and select an alert style.

12 Click OK.

Sorting table data

Sorting is one of the most effective tools Excel gives you to help interpret data. Sorting allows you to reorganise the information you have recorded so you can view it according to a pattern. Ascending order sorts records from A to Z, earliest to latest, or lowest to highest. Descending order does the reverse – Z to A, and so on.

1 Click the table cell that has the field name by which you want to sort.

2 Click the Data tab.

3 Click one of the sort buttons, Sort Ascending or Sort Descending.

4 If you need to reapply the sort to other cells in the table, click the Reapply button.

? **DID YOU KNOW?**

You can also sort a list using one or more sort fields – fields you select to help arrange list data. Suppose you have arranged one record, or one set of cells, using the sort criteria you want to use. You can select the cell and then click the Sort button to sort by those attributes.

Analysing data with a PivotTable or PivotChart

A PivotTable is an ideal tool for summarising data using complex criteria. A PivotTable lets you quickly select the fields and criteria you want to use to present in the table. You can also format the table as a table, or make the data easier to read by formatting it as a PivotChart.

1 Click anywhere in the table or select a range of cells.

2 Click the Insert tab.

3 Click the PivotTable down arrow, and select PivotTable or PivotChart.

4 From the dialogue box, click the Select a table or range option, or click Use an external data source, click Choose Connection and select a connection to a remote file.

5 Select either the New Worksheet or Existing Worksheet option.

6 Click OK.

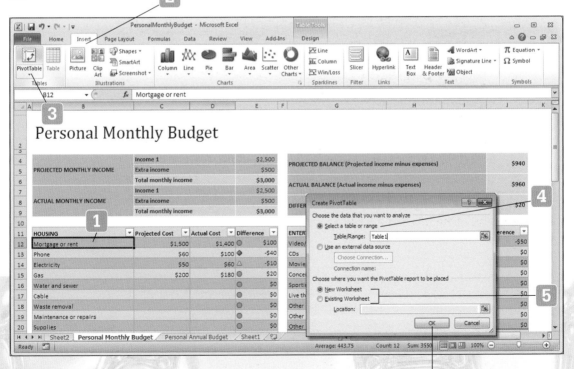

7 Select the check boxes next to the fields you want to include in the PivotTable.

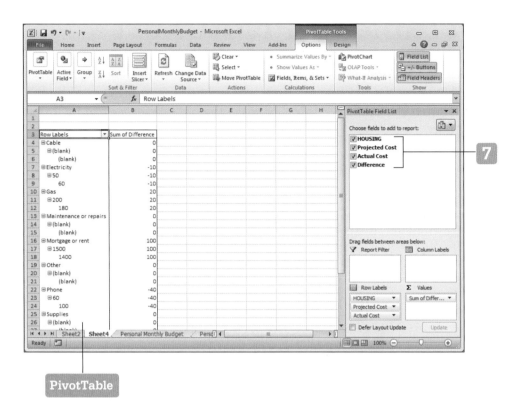

PivotTable

? DID YOU KNOW?

When you're done with your PivotTable, you can delete it by clicking the Options tab, clicking the Select button, clicking Entire PivotTable and pressing Delete.

Update a PivotTable

Once you create a PivotTable, it's particularly easy to modify its contents. You can use the PivotTable Field List or the Options tab under PivotTable Tools. By using these options, you don't have to recreate the title whenever you want to add new data to it.

1 Click any cell in the PivotTable.

2 Select or clear the check boxes in the PivotTable Field List.

3 To reorder the position of a field, drag its name in the Field List to one of the other boxes.

4 Click Update to refresh the report layout.

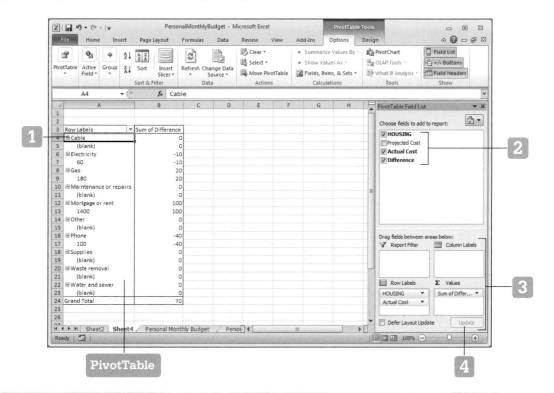

PivotTable

? DID YOU KNOW?

The PivotTable Tools heading only appears when you have clicked inside a PivotTable.

Convert text to columns

Excel provides you with an easy-to-use wizard that leads you through the process of separating the contents of cells into separate columns. For instance, if a cell contains a series of numbers, you can use the wizard to separate each number into its own column.

1 Select the range of cells you want to convert into columns.

2 Click the Data tab.

3 Click the Text to Columns button.

4 From the Convert Text to Column Wizard dialogue box, select the Delimited option.

5 Click Next.

6 From the Delimiters group box, select the type of delimiter options you want to use. Follow the rest of the steps in the wizard.

7 Click Finish.

? DID YOU KNOW?

The options shown in the wizard differ depending on the type of delimiter being used to separate the cells' contents into separate columns.

Create an outline

Excel data can be formatted as an outline, which presents a hierarchical set of information that is easy to interpret. A set of data in outline form consists of items that can have multiple topics or levels of information within them.

1 Organise a set of data in hierarchical fashion.

2 Select the data you want to convert into an outline.

3 Click the Data tab.

4 Click the Group button, and then select Auto Outline from the drop-down list.

HOT TIP: When creating data for an outline, place summary rows below detail rows and summary columns to the right of detail columns.

7 Creating and modifying graphics and shapes

Introduction

In the previous chapters you have learned about analysing and interpreting data, and formatting, tables and colour themes. Now you're ready to explore the many options Excel gives you for working with graphics that can make your worksheets look professional and visually appealing. Anything you can do to make the data in your Excel spreadsheets easier to interpret will make your work more valuable to your colleagues.

Since Excel is part of Microsoft Office, you gain access to the extensive library of Clip Art that comes with the application suite. You can also browse through Clip Art that Microsoft makes available to Office users online. Once you add a graphic image, you can resize, recolour and crop it as you would in any other Office application.

Simple graphic images will enhance your worksheets, but Excel also includes the ability to add specialised objects. WordArt is a feature that can enhance labels and titles and that comes with many style choices. You can also insert SmartArt graphics to illustrate a sequence of steps in a process, or the relationships between points of information.

Locate and insert Clip Art

When you need an image for a worksheet, the quickest option is to add Clip Art. Clip Art is artwork that has been made available by its creators for use by others. An extensive library is available to users of Excel and other Office applications. You search for it through the Clip Art task pane, and browse for the image you want in a library called the Clip Organiser.

1 Click the Insert tab.

2 Click the Clip Art button. The Clip Art task pane opens.

3 Type a keyword or phrase that describes the image you want.

4 Click the Results should be arrow to limit the search to a particular collection.

5 Select the Include Office.com content check box.

6 Click Go or press Enter.

7 Double-click the image you want to add to the current Excel document.

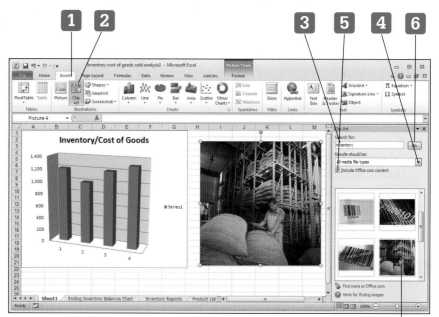

Resize and move an image

Most of the images in the Clip Organiser are initially far too big in width and depth to be accommodated in their entirety in a worksheet. You need to resize them to make them fit alongside any charts or tables you have created.

1 Click one of the resize handles around the image you have inserted.

2 Drag the image toward its centre to make it smaller; drag it outward to enlarge it.

3 When you're done, release the mouse button.

4 Click on the image while holding down the mouse button and drag it to move it anywhere in the current worksheet.

5 When the image is positioned correctly, release the mouse button.

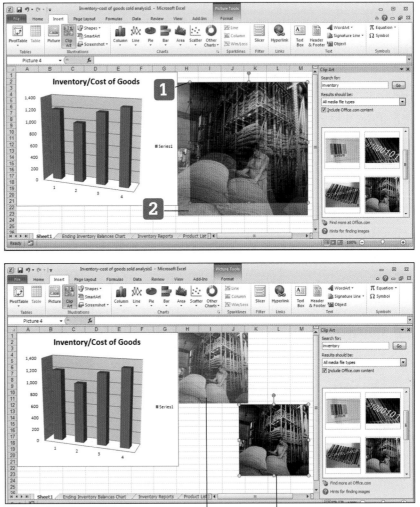

ALERT: If you don't want to distort the image by changing the ratio of width to height, press and hold down the Shift key as you resize.

Find more Clip Art online

The Clip Organiser is extensive, but it might not have the image you are looking for. To search a wider range of possibilities, you can go to Microsoft Office Online. This is a website that Microsoft makes available to its customers so they can browse and insert Clip Art.

1 Click the Insert tab.

2 Click the Clip Art button. The Clip Art task pane opens.

3 Click the Find more at Office.com link. Your web browser opens (if it isn't open already). It connects to the Microsoft Office Online Clip Art home page.

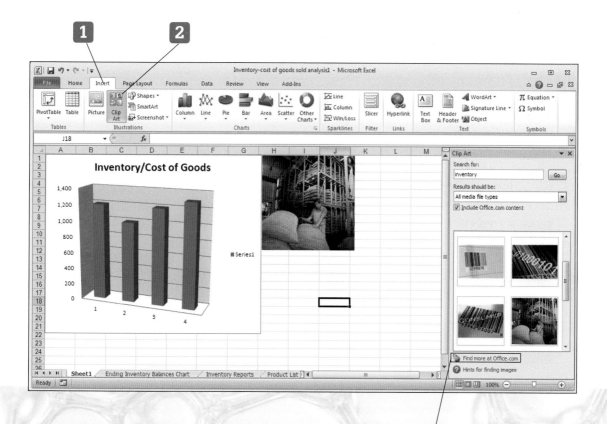

4 Type your search criteria in the search field.

5 Select the media type you want to find.

6 Click Search.

7 When you find an image, place your mouse over the image and select an option such as Copy to Clipboard or Add to Basket. If you add the image to the selection basket, click on the Selection Basket link to download the image.

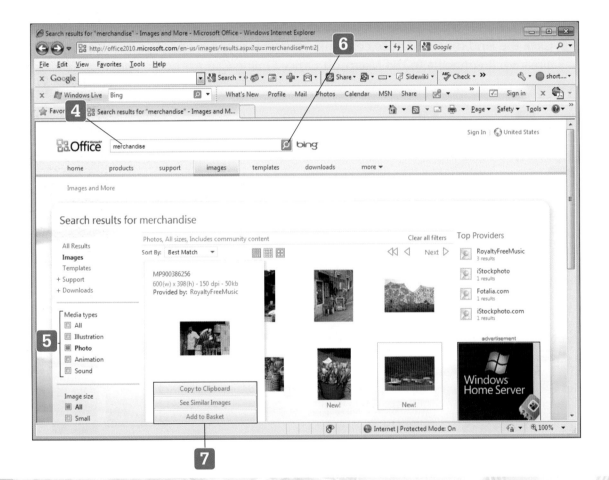

ALERT: You have to be connected to the Internet in order to access Microsoft Office Online.

Dividing Clip Art into categories

The images that come with the Clip Organiser are organised in their own categories. But you might want to set aside some images for your own use, particularly if they apply to on-going projects. In this way, you can assemble your own personal collection of Clip Art images.

1 Click Start, and then click Programs or All Programs.

2 Click Microsoft Office.

3 Click Microsoft Office 2010 Tools.

4 Select Microsoft Clip Organizer from the list.

5 Click the File menu in the Clip Organizer, select Add Clips to Organizer and then select On My Own.

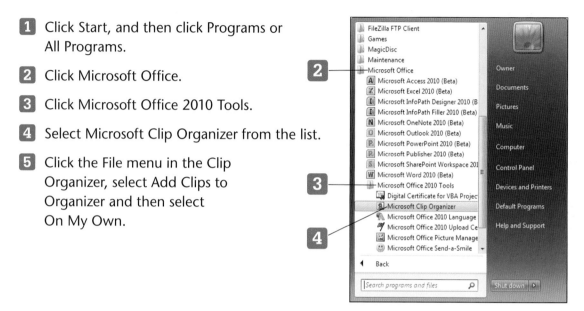

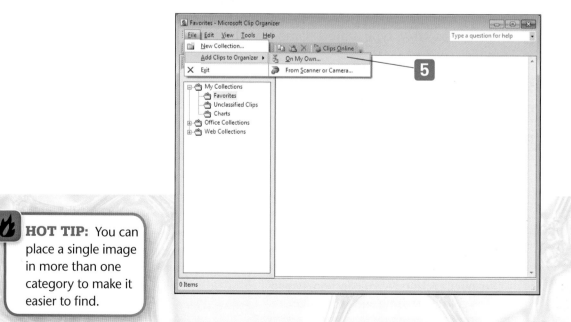

HOT TIP: You can place a single image in more than one category to make it easier to find.

6 Locate the clip you want to add, and click the image to select it.

7 Click the Add To button.

8 Select the collection to which you want to add the clip.

9 Click New to create a new folder that describes the artwork you are gathering.

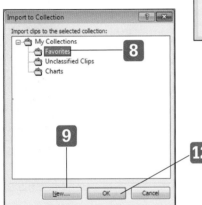

10 If you clicked New, type a short name that clearly identifies your artwork.

11 Click OK.

12 Click OK.

13 Click Add.

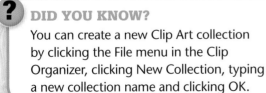

Change Clip Art properties

You don't have to use clip art 'as is'. You can move it, change its name or add keywords to it that make it easier to find when you're doing a search.

1 Click Start, and then click Programs or All Programs.

2 Click Microsoft Office.

3 Click Microsoft Office 2010 Tools.

4 Select Microsoft Clip Organizer from the list.

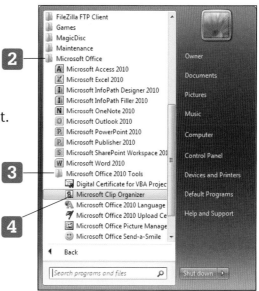

5 In the Clip Organizer, point to the clip you want to categorise, click the list arrow and select one of the available options:

- Copy to Collection lets you place a copy of the image to another category.

- Move to Collection lets you move the clip to a different category.

- Edit Keywords lets you add descriptive keywords to the image.

6 Select Preview/Properties to view current information about the image and change keywords.

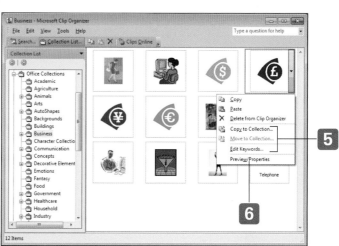

ALERT: In order to add a caption to the image or edit the keywords currently associated with it, you need to move it to the My Collections area of the Clip Organizer.

7 Review the file size, physical size, file format and other properties.

8 Click Edit Keywords to change the keywords associated with the file.

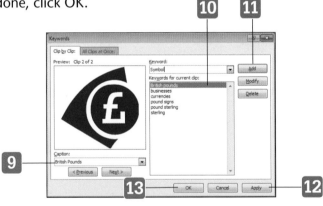

9 Type a caption for the image in the Caption field.

10 Type a keyword for the image in the Keyword field.

11 Click Add.

12 Click Apply if you want to save the current changes without closing the dialogue box.

13 When you're done, click OK.

? DID YOU KNOW?

You can also change image properties in the Clip Art task pane. Pass your mouse pointer over an image, click the down arrow next to the clip, and click one of the options shown (Copy to Collection, Move to Collection, Edit Keywords and Delete from Clip Organizer.)

Adding artwork to the Clip Organizer

The Clip Organizer isn't just a repository for Clip Art provided by Microsoft. You can also use it to collect and arrange your own artwork – your own photos and drawings and artwork you have either generated yourself or had created for your office (such as your company's logo).

1 Click Start, and then click Programs or All Programs.

2 Click Microsoft Office.

3 Click Microsoft Office 2010 Tools.

4 Select Microsoft Clip Organizer from the list.

5 Click the File menu, point to Add Clips to Organizer and click On My Own.

6 Click the Look in down arrow, and select the folder on your file system that contains the image you want to add.

7 Click the File as type down arrow, and select the type of file you want to view.

8 Click the image(s) you want to import.

9 Click Add.

Remove artwork from the Clip Organizer

The Clip Organizer can quickly become crowded with files. If you no longer need an image stored in the Organizer, you can remove it, which will make the application less crowded and save disk space.

1 Follow steps 1 to 4 in the preceding section to open the Clip Organizer.

2 Click the down arrow next to the image you want to remove.

3 Select Delete from Clip Organizer drop-down list to remove the Clip Art from all categories in the Clip Organizer.

4 Click OK when prompted to remove the artwork from the Clip Organizer. Or click Cancel to keep the artwork in the Clip Organizer.

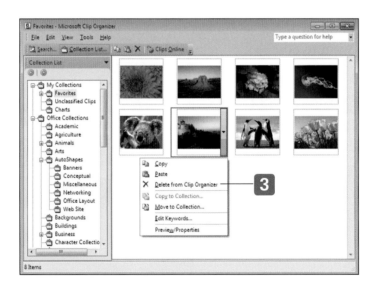

? DID YOU KNOW?

Most of the Clip Art contained in the Clip Organizer is created and stored in the Windows Media Format, which has the .wmf file extension. This format, like other graphic formats, compresses image files to conserve disk space. You might still encounter a file (particularly a photographic image) that consumes lots of space and that should be removed.

Scale an image

Page layouts can quickly become complex and crowded. At the same time, it's important to use white space effectively in order to maintain a professional-looking design. It can be helpful to scale an image: to change its size with precision to fit a predefined space instead of dragging it, which is quicker but less precise.

1 Click the image you want to resize.

2 Click the Format tab.

3 Click the Size dialogue box launcher.

4 In the format Picture dialogue box, select the Lock aspect ratio check box to maintain the image's height and width so it doesn't get distorted.

5 Click the up and down arrows to enter a size, or type numbers in the Height and Width boxes.

6 Click Close.

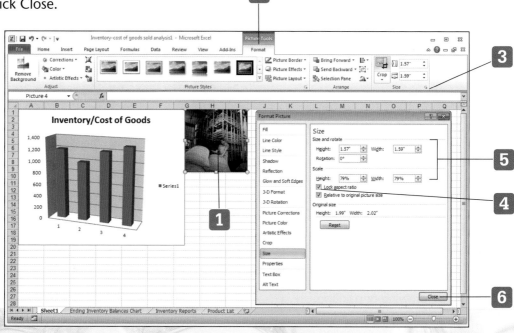

SEE ALSO: See 'Resize and move an image' earlier in this chapter for instructions on how to drag an image's handles to change its size.

? DID YOU KNOW?

You can enter a numeric size in the Size boxes or a percentage size in the Scale boxes in the Format Pictures dialogue box.

Change brightness and contrast

Brightness and contrast are two of the most common and effective adjustments you can make to any image. These controls appear under Picture Tools, which only appears when you select an image.

1 Click the image you want to adjust.

2 Click the Format tab.

3 Click the Corrections button, and do one of the following:

- Select Sharpen and Soften to change the blurriness or fuzziness of the image.

- Select Brightness and Contrast to increase or decrease how light or how dark the image looks.

- Select Picture Corrections Options to adjust brightness interactively using a slider tool.

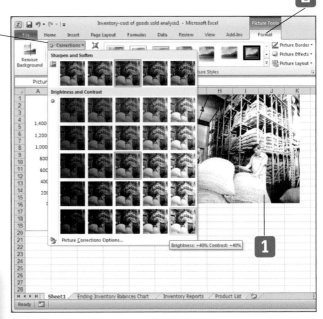

Draw a shape

You don't want to make your worksheets look unprofessional by drawing a clumsy or amateurish image atop your nicely arranged data. Excel helps by supplying ready-made shapes you can insert with a few mouse clicks and then edit as needed.

1 Click the Insert tab.

2 Click the Shapes button.

3 Click the shape you want from the Shapes gallery.

4 Drag the cursor (which appears as a plus sign) down and to the right to draw the image.

5 Release the mouse button when you are done.

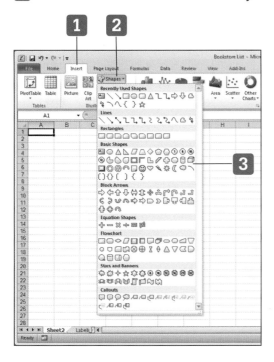

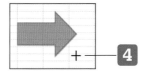

🔥 **HOT TIP:** Hold down the Shift key as you draw to maintain the proportions of the shape you draw.

❓ **DID YOU KNOW?**
Most Excel shapes come with an adjustment handle you can drag to make the image larger or smaller.

Resize a shape

Once you insert a shape, you are free to resize it as you would any other image. You can drag the image using one of the resize handles. You can also change the size to a precise measurement using the Size dialogue box launcher.

1 Select the shape you want to resize.

2 Drag one of the sizing handles to resize the image.

3 Click the rotate handle to 'spin' the image.

4 Click the Size dialogue box launcher to scale the image with precision.

5 Use the controls to change the image size.

6 Click Close.

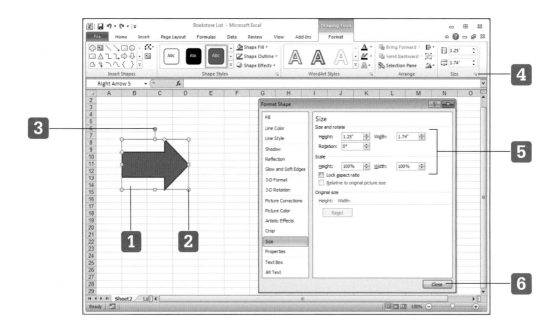

HOT TIP: To delete a shape, select it and then press the Delete (Del) key.

Add text to a shape

Captions and labels make data in a worksheet easier to interpret. Shapes can be easier to interpret by adding text. You can add text to a shape just as you would any text box. Select the shape object and start typing.

1 Select the shape that you want to contain the text.

2 On the Format tab, click the Text Box button.

3 Click the image and type the text you want.

4 To make text corrections, click anywhere in the text to position the cursor, and then edit the characters.

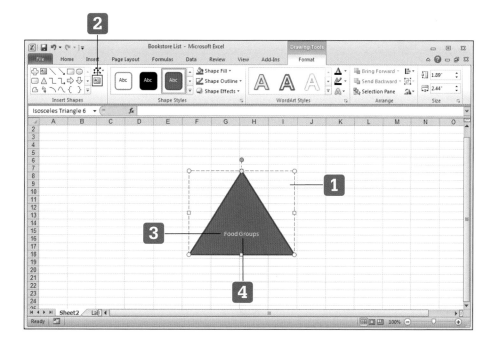

? DID YOU KNOW?

When you place text in a shape, the text becomes part of the object, and will move and resize along with the object.

? DID YOU KNOW?

You can use the text formatting tools on the Home tab to make a text block bold or italic, or to change the size.

Draw a line or arrow

Lines and arrows are popular shapes you can add to your spreadsheets. They are perfect for illustrating trends or for directing the viewer's attention to important contents. Both can be found in the Shapes gallery.

1 Click the Insert tab.

2 Click the Shapes button, and select a shape from the drop-down list.

3 Drag the pointer to draw a line or arrow. The locations of the endpoints depend on where you start and stop dragging.

4 Release the mouse button when you're done, and use the resize handles to move or resize the line or arrow as needed.

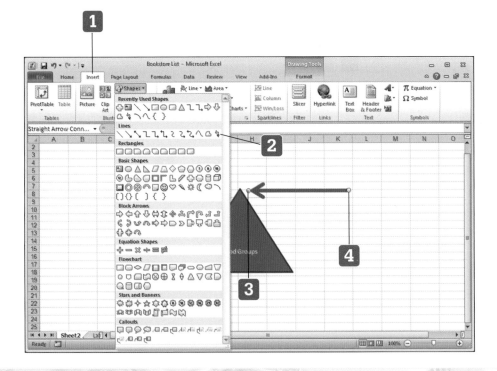

Apply a Quick Style to a line

You can always format a line, arrow or other shape by using the formatting tools on the Home tab or on the Format tab under Picture tools. But you'll save time adding multiple formatting attributes to a line or arrow by applying Shape Quick Styles.

1 Click the shape you want to format.

2 Click the Format tab.

3 Scan the Shapes Styles tool group for colours and styles. Click the scroll up or down arrows or the More down arrow to view additional options.

4 Pass your mouse pointer over a style to view a live preview in the current shape.

5 Click the style you want from the gallery to select it.

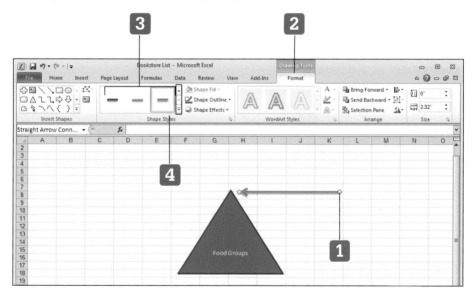

? DID YOU KNOW?

You can also modify a shape by using other options on the Format tab, such as the Shape Outline or Shape Fill buttons.

? DID YOU KNOW?

Each style in the gallery has a name (such as Accent 1), which appears as a tool tip when your mouse hovers over the style.

Copy or move an object

Once you create, edit, scale and style a shape or other object, you'll probably need to move or copy it to a new location at some point. You have two options: you can drag the object with your mouse, or use the Size and Position dialogue box to precisely position it.

1 To use your mouse, drag the object to move it, or press and hold down the Ctrl key while dragging the object to copy it.

2 To use Excel's menus, select the object(s) you want to copy or move.

3 Click the Home tab.

4 Click the Copy or Cut button.

5 Click in the location where you want the object(s) to be moved, whether it is in the same worksheet or a different one.

6 Click the Paste button.

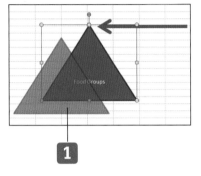

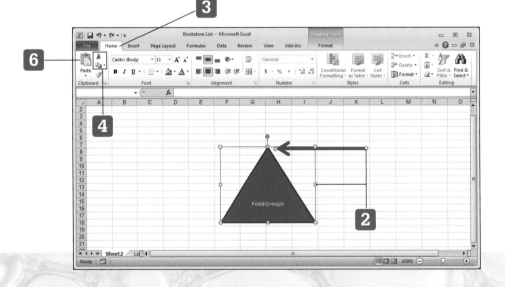

 DID YOU KNOW?
You can copy objects to the Office Clipboard and then paste them to other parts of the same workbook or different workbooks, or even other Office documents.

HOT TIP: Press Shift+Click to select multiple objects so you can move or copy them together.

Fill an object with colour

The Format tab under Picture Tools gives you a variety of ways to quickly add formatting to shapes that complements the data in the rest of your worksheet. Two controls you should take advantage of are the Shape Fill button and the Fill section of the Format Shape dialogue box.

1 Select the shape you want to format.

2 Click the Format tab.

3 Click the Shape Fill button.

4 Select a colour you want from the palette.

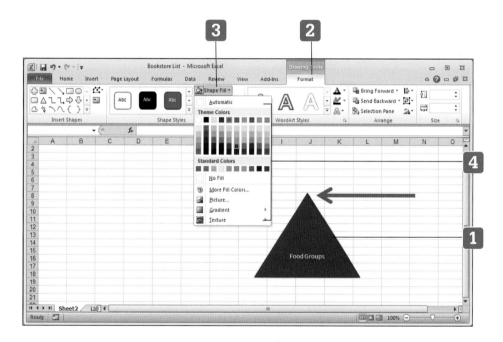

? DID YOU KNOW?
You can specify a colour and line style as a default. Right-click the object and select Set as Default Shape from the context menu.

🔥 HOT TIP: To remove a colour fill, click the Shape Fill button and then click No Fill.

Distribute objects

Excel gives you grids and guides to align objects to a specific position. The Align commands under the Format tab enable you to position the objects in relation to one another or to other contents in your worksheet.

1 Select the objects you want to position.

2 Click the Format tab.

3 Click the Align button and select one of the following:

- Click Snap to Grid to align the objects relative to the worksheet's grid.

- Click Snap to Shape if you want to align the objects relative to each other.

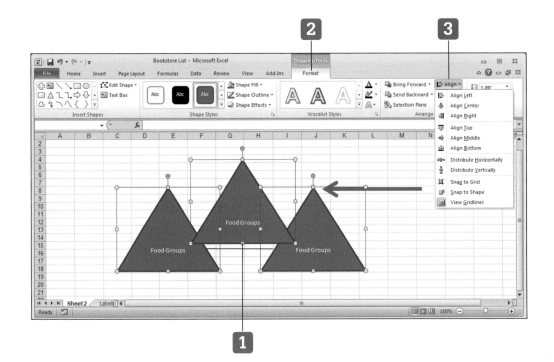

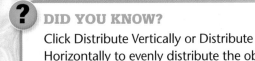

8 Publishing workbooks and worksheets

Introduction

In the previous chapters, you have learned how to analyse and interpret data, format tables and work with graphics to make your worksheets look professional and visually appealing.

Once you complete a worksheet, you'll want to make it available to the people who need to work with it. Excel makes it easy for you to format documents and preview them so they print exactly the way you want. You also have the option to control what appears on any given page by inserting page breaks as well as headers and footers.

When you're ready to print a document, you can select to print an entire worksheet or only part of it. That enables you to produce a range of content for each audience that needs it. The Print dialogue box lets you select a print range and print area as well. You can also distribute your data to others who don't have Excel by converting it to PDF or XPS format; both are secure fixed-layout formats.

These days, one of the most frequently used publishing options involves creating webpages. Excel gives you the tools you need to create webpages from your workbooks and to optimise them for publication on the Web. You can save your files in HyperText Markup Language (HTML) format using the Save As command. You can also add and format hyperlinks, which allow users to jump from one part of a worksheet to another one or to another location on the Web. Using the Web is a great way to share data with others and add research-based information to your worksheets as well.

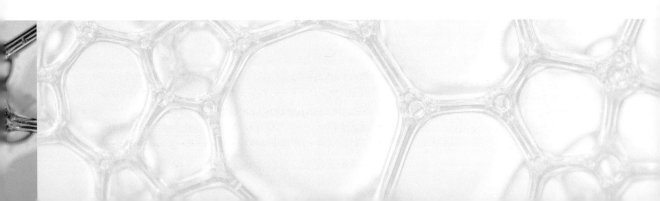

Configure page size and orientation

Before you print or otherwise publish an Excel worksheet, you need to set up the page size and orientation so it looks the way you want. You have the ability to change page orientation in Page Layout View. The Page Layout tab lets you adjust the page size quickly without opening a special dialogue box.

1 Click the Page Layout tab.

2 Click the Orientation button.

3 Select Portrait for vertically oriented printing or Landscape for horizontally oriented printing.

? DID YOU KNOW?

You can print any comments you have added to files. First click the Page Layout tab. Then click the Page Setup dialogue box launcher, click the Sheet tab, click the down arrow next to Comments, click As displayed on sheet or At end of sheet, and finally click Print.

Customise page size

If you want more control over the size of your page than the Orientation button gives you, you can always turn to the Page Setup dialogue box. You'll find a full range of paper sizes used both in the UK and elsewhere. You can also adjust features such as print quantity as well.

1 Click the Page Layout tab.

2 Click the Size button.

3 Select More Paper Sizes option. The Page Setup dialogue box opens.

4 Select a paper size from the Paper size drop-down list.

5 Select the print quality from the Print quality drop-down list.

6 Click the Print button.

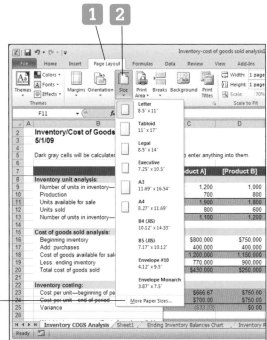

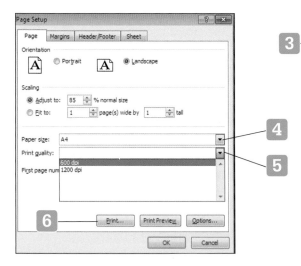

! ALERT: The higher the print quality you select, the slower your printing will be, and the more printer toner you will use.

? DID YOU KNOW?
You can also use the Page Setup dialogue box to adjust print scaling, which is the process of enlarging or reducing the size of a printed page.

Adjust page margins

Page Margins are the blank areas between the printed contents and the edge of the paper. You set up page margins to determine how much content each page can hold, and how readable the page is.

1 Click the Page Layout tab.

2 Click the Margins button.

3 Select an option you want from the drop-down list.

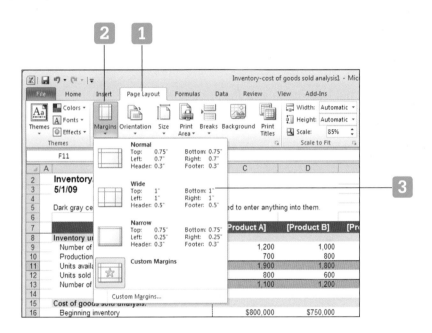

? DID YOU KNOW?

The current margin setting is highlighted under the Margins button menu.

? DID YOU KNOW?

You can also use the mouse pointer to adjust margins interactively for the entire document while you are in Page Layout View. Click the Page Layout View button on the View tab.

Use the ruler to adjust margins

If you use the ruler to adjust margins for the current worksheet, you gain the ability to adjust any tab settings as well, and you can see the changes interactively as you make them.

1 Click the View tab.

2 Click the Page Layout button.

3 Select the Ruler check box.

4 Position the cursor over the left, right, top or bottom edge of the ruler until the mouse pointer changes to a double arrow.

5 Drag to adjust the margin setting.

6 Click the Normal button to exit Page Layout View.

HOT TIP: As you move the edge of the ruler, a ScreenTip appears to indicate the margin name and current position.

Customise margin settings

You aren't limited to the margin settings that appear when you click the Margins button on the Page Layout tab. If you want to use a non-standard margin setting, you can specify your own custom margins.

1 Click the Page Layout tab.

2 Click the Margins button, and click Custom Margins. The Page Setup dialogue box opens with the Margins tab in front.

3 Click the Top, Bottom, Left and Right up or down arrows to change the margins.

4 Select the Horizontally or Vertically check box to centre the content on the page.

5 Click OK.

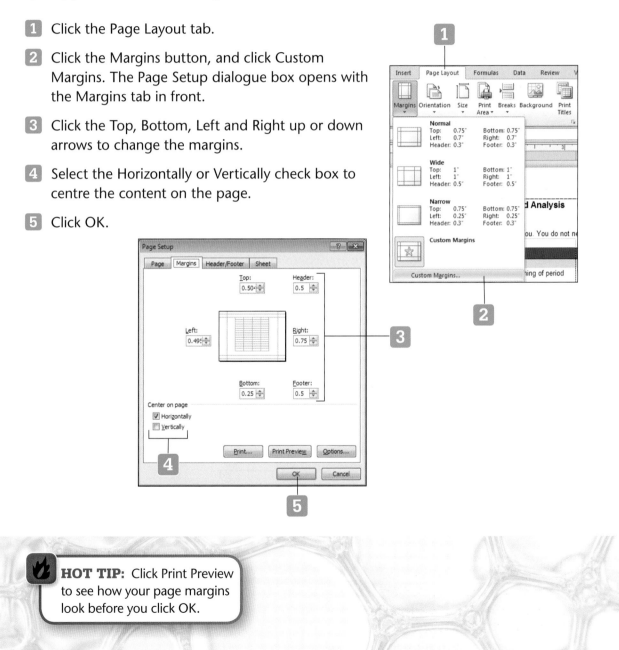

HOT TIP: Click Print Preview to see how your page margins look before you click OK.

Create headers and footers

Headers and footers are areas of the page between the main contents and the margins. They contain supplementary information about a file such as page numbers. They make your files easier for readers to follow. Excel lets you quickly add predefined header or footer with just a few mouse clicks.

1 Click the Insert tab.

2 Click the Header & Footer button. The worksheet opens in Page Layout View.

3 Click the Header or Footer button, and then select the type of information you want.

4 Type the text you want to add about the file.

5 To close headers or footers, click anywhere in the worksheet or press Esc.

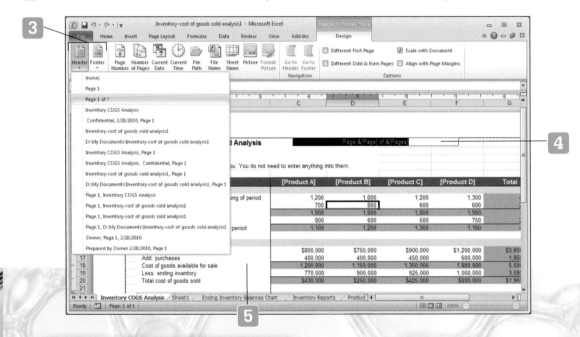

? DID YOU KNOW?

A header is located at the top of a page, and a footer is located at the bottom.

Insert a page break

Page breaks control the arrangements of data on worksheets that are larger than a printed page. If you don't insert a manual page break, Excel inserts automatic page breaks for you. But if you don't like the location of the automatic page break, you can set your own.

1 Select the location where you want to insert a page break:

- Horizontal. To create a horizontal page break, click the row where you want to insert it.

- Vertical. To create a vertical page break, click the column where you want it to appear.

- Cell. To insert a horizontal and vertical page break at the same time, click the cell below and to the right of where you want the break to occur.

2 Click the Page Layout tab.

3 Click the Breaks button, and select Insert Page Break.

Screenshot of Microsoft Excel showing the Page Layout tab with the Breaks button menu open, displaying options: Insert Page Break, Remove Page Break, Reset All Page Breaks. The worksheet shows "Inventory/Cost of Goods Sold Analysis" data.

? **DID YOU KNOW?**

You can see breaks before they are printed; they appear as dotted lines on the worksheet.

Specify the print area

When you are ready to print a worksheet, you can select exactly how much of the document you want to print. Doing so can save you a lot of wasted toner and paper. The print area is the part of your worksheet that Excel will send to the printer.

1 Select the range of cells you want to print.

2 Click the Page Layout tab.

3 Click the Print Area button, and then select Set Print Area.

? DID YOU KNOW?

You can expand a print area by clicking the cell where you want to extend the print area. Click Page Layout, click the Print Area button and then select Add to Print Area.

🔥 HOT TIP: To clear a print area, click the Print Area button and select Clear Print Area.

Preview a worksheet before printing

Even after you have set margins, specified the page size and chosen the area of the worksheet you want to print, you have one more chance to check the document before it is printed. It's a good idea to verify that the page looks the way you want to save time, toner and paper. Print Preview shows you how your document will look when it prints.

1 Click the File tab.

2 Click Print.

3 Click the Show Margins button to adjust margins visually.

4 Click any tab on the ribbon to return to the worksheet without printing.

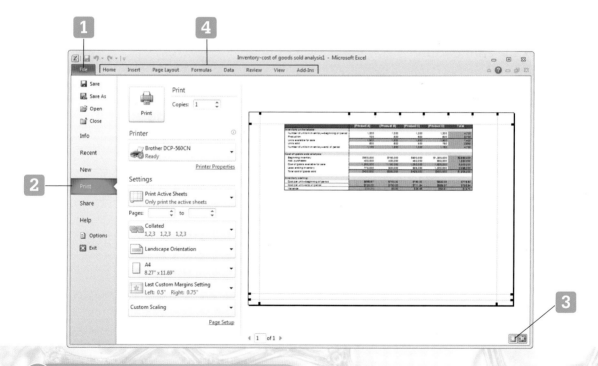

? DID YOU KNOW?

You can zoom in and out to view data more easily on the Zoom to Page button next to the Show Margins button in the lower right-hand corner of the window.

Print a worksheet

When you have set your margins and the print area and previewed your worksheet, you're ready to print it. You have the option to print all or part of the worksheet or select the secondary features that you want printed, such as gridlines, column letters or row numbers.

1 Click the File tab.

2 Click Print.

3 Select a printer from the Printer drop-down list.

4 Specify the number of copies you want.

5 Select whether you want to print the entire document or just a page range.

6 To change the printer properties (to print in grayscale, for instance), click the Printer Properties link.

7 Click the Print button.

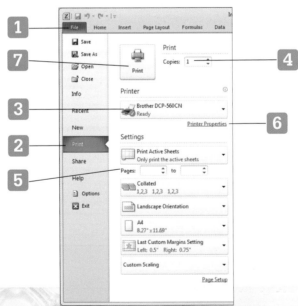

? DID YOU KNOW?

You can print a copy of your worksheet without first opening the Print dialogue box. Just select the Quick Print button on the quick access toolbar.

🔥 HOT TIP: Press Ctrl+P to open the Print dialogue box immediately.

Create a PDF file

PDF is a commonly used abbreviation for Portable Document Format, a file format created by Adobe Systems for its PageMaker and other files. It compresses files, preserves complex layouts, embeds non-standard fonts and includes images, all in a compact package that can be quickly transmitted over the Internet or another network.

1. Click the File tab.

2. Click Save As. The Save As dialogue box appears.

3. Select the location where you want to save the file.

4. Type a file name for the PDF file.

5. Select PDF from the Save as type drop-down list.

6. If you want to open the file after saving it, select the Open file after Publishing check box.

7. Click the Options button, select the publishing options, and click OK.

8. Click Save.

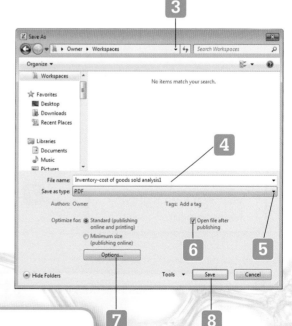

? DID YOU KNOW?

If you don't see the PDF option when you point to Save As, you need to download an add-in. To add the missing add-in, click the file tab, click Options and select Add-Ins for other formats.

? DID YOU KNOW?

To view a PDF file, you or your colleagues need to have Adobe Reader, a free reader program you can download from the Adobe website, http://www.adobe.com.

Create an XPS document

XPS stands for XML Paper Specification. It is a secure fixed-layout format created by Microsoft that lets you retain the form you intended when a file is sent to a printer or a monitor. XPS is a good option if you are preparing a file to be printed on paper without modification.

1 Click the File tab.

2 Click Save As. The Save As dialogue box appears.

3 Select the location where you want to save the file.

4 Type a file name for the XPS file.

5 Select XPS Document from the Save as type drop-down list.

6 If you want to open the file after saving it, select the Open file after publishing check box.

7 Click the Options button, select the publishing options, and click OK.

8 Click Save.

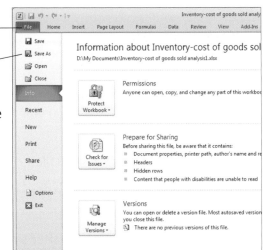

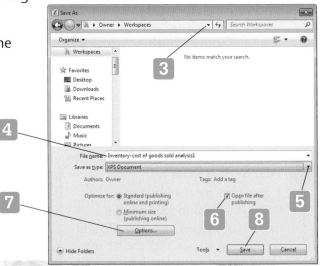

? DID YOU KNOW?

XPS format preserves live links with documents. It is also compatible with Windows Rights Management.

! ALERT: If you don't see XPS listed on the Save As menu, you need to download the Office add-in for saving a file as XPS. Install it from the Microsoft Download Centre.

Save a workbook as a webpage

One of the most popular ways to publish a file is to save it as a webpage. That way anyone can view it in the Internet or your local network with a web browser. When you save an Excel document as a webpage you convert it to HyperText Markup Language (HTML) format.

1 Click the File tab.

2 Click Save As. The Save As dialogue box appears.

3 Select the location where you want to save the file.

4 Type a file name for the file.

5 Select Web Page from the Save as type drop-down list.

6 Click the Change Title button to add a title for the webpage and click OK.

7 Click Save.

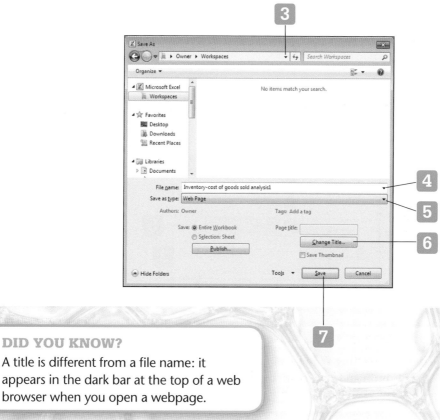

? DID YOU KNOW?

A title is different from a file name: it appears in the dark bar at the top of a web browser when you open a webpage.

Open a workbook in webpage format

Excel isn't a web browser, but it has the ability to open a worksheet that you previously saved as a webpage. Opening the worksheet as a webpage allows you to quickly switch from HTML to standard Excel format without losing any functionality.

1 Click the File tab.

2 Click Open. The Open dialogue box appears.

3 Select All Web Pages from the file type drop-down list.

4 Click the Look in down arrow to locate the webpage file you want to open.

5 Click the file to select it.

6 Click Open.

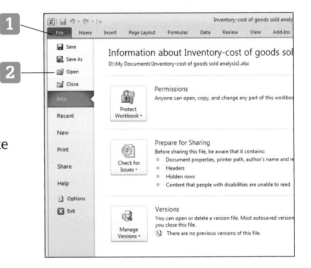

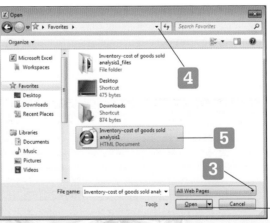

HOT TIP: If you want to open the file in your web browser rather than Excel, click the Open button and select Open in Browser.

Preview a webpage

Before you open a worksheet as a webpage, and before you even save it as a webpage, you can get a preview of how it would look on the Web. By previewing the file you can see if there are any errors that needed to be corrected before they appear online.

1 Open the workbook you want to preview.

2 Click the Web Page Preview button on the quick access toolbar. Your default web browser opens and displays the document as a webpage.

3 Click the Close button to close your browser window.

> **ALERT:** If you don't see the Web Page Preview button on the quick access toolbar, you'll need to add it. Click the quick access toolbar, select More Commands and add the Web Page Preview button.

Create a hyperlink

An Excel worksheet can contain links to specific sites on the Internet. Such links enable you and your colleagues to jump to resources that are related to the data you are presenting.

1 Select the cell, object or text that you want to convert to a hyperlink.

2 Click the Insert tab.

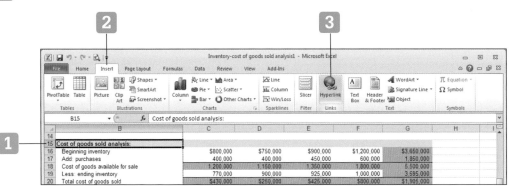

3 Click the Hyperlink button.

4 In the Link to section (left pane), click one of the buttons to select the type of link you want to create.

5 Type or select the name and location of the webpage you want to link to.

6 Click OK.

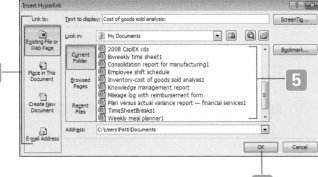

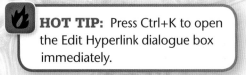 **HOT TIP:** Press Ctrl+K to open the Edit Hyperlink dialogue box immediately.

? DID YOU KNOW?

When your worksheet contains a hyperlink, it is formatted in a cell as blue text.

Format a hyperlink

Excel provides you with extensive options for formatting many kinds of data types, including hyperlinks. It pays to format hyperlinks clearly so viewers know they are clicking on a link and aren't surprised when a web browser opens.

1 Click the Home tab.

2 Click the Cell Styles button.

3 Right-click the Linked Cell option and select Modify.

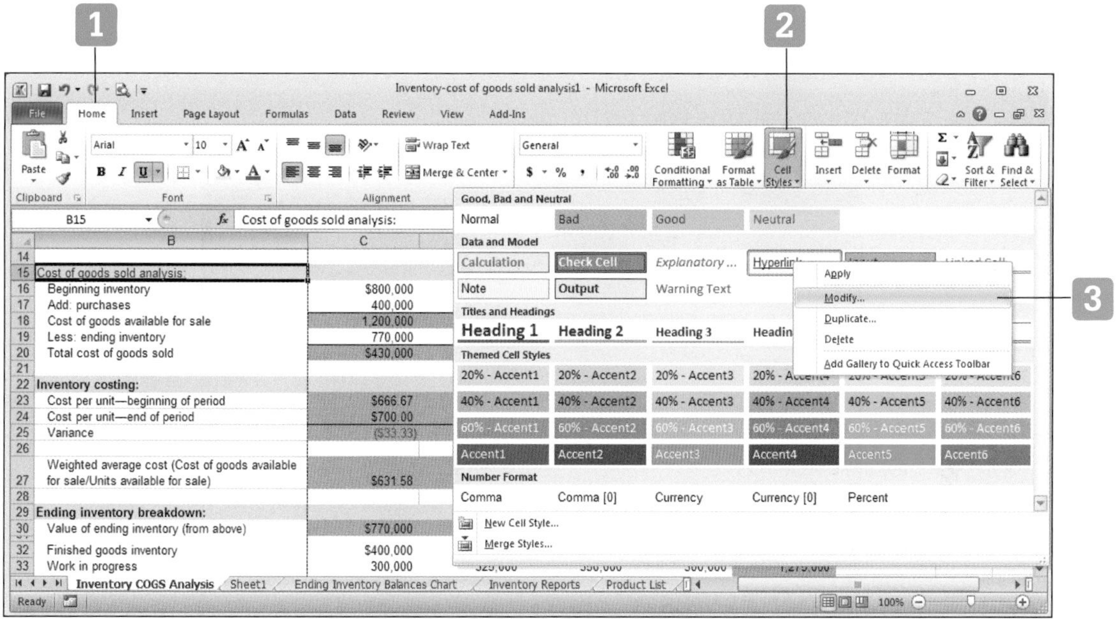

? DID YOU KNOW?

You can copy or move a hyperlink. Right-click the hyperlink you want to copy or move, and select Copy or Cut from the context menu. Right-click the cell you want to contain the link and select Paste from the context menu.

4 Click the Format button.

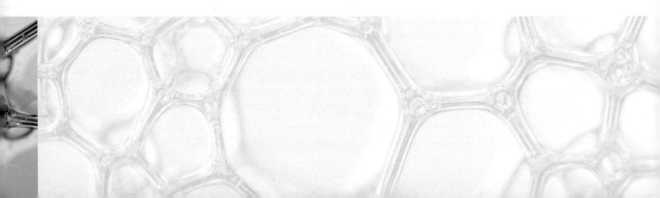

5 Select the formatting options you want.

6 Click OK.

9 Protecting and securing your data

Introduction

In the previous chapter, you learned how to customise and configure your worksheet page size. You also learned how to save your worksheet in different formats such as PDF, XPS and webpages. Now you're ready to protect and secure your data.

Much of the information you will gather and present with Microsoft Excel 2010 is financial – budgets, expenses, projections, salaries and other records. No matter whether you're working in an office or keeping records for your household, it's a good idea to protect your worksheet data so that unauthorised individuals cannot gain access to it.

It's also important to be able to choose and control which content is displayed and which is protected, and Excel gives you many layers of control over what you restrict. You can lock individual cells so they cannot be changed; you can password-protect a worksheet or an entire workbook. You can also encrypt workbooks – or all of the above. You have the option to implement many layers of control or just one, depending on your needs.

This chapter examines common security options available to Excel 2010 users. You can set security options at the Trust Center. That's also where you'll find technology information that relates to document privacy, safety and security from Microsoft. In this chapter you'll find out how to make the most of the Trust Center. Other features such as digital signatures and encryption are particularly powerful additions to this version of Excel; they ensure that your data can't be accessed without authorisation even if you send it to someone else over the Internet.

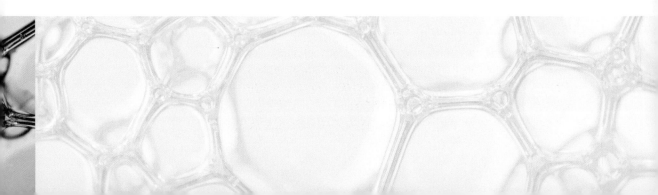

Protect a worksheet

Passwords can be used to protect a worksheet. That way you won't have to worry about losing your hard work if others have access to your files. You're probably already familiar with the drill. You supply your password, and then you enter it again when you want to work on the file.

1 Click the Review tab.

2 Click the Protect Sheet button.

3 Select the check boxes for the options you want protected. If you don't want an option protected, then click the option to clear it.

4 Type a password to prevent users from undoing your protection.

5 Click OK.

6 Retype the password.

7 Click OK.

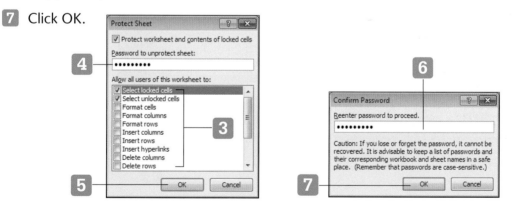

HOT TIP: Be sure to remember or write down your password(s), because you won't be able to open your files if you forget. They are case sensitive, so you have to supply them exactly as they were first entered.

Lock and unlock worksheet cells

If you don't want to bother with a password but do want to make sure that changes to your data can't be made accidently, you can lock your worksheet cells.

1 Select the cell or range you want to lock or unlock.

2 Click the Home tab.

3 Click the Format button.

4 Select Lock Cell from the drop-down list to lock or unlock the current selection.

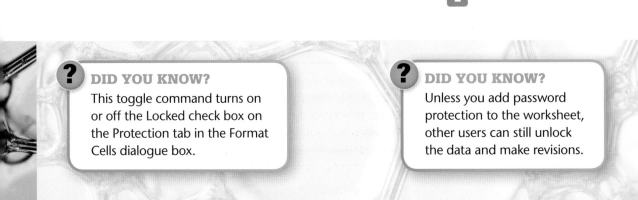

Lock other worksheet elements

Sometimes, you want others in your organisation to be able to view or edit workbooks, while protecting data in parts of the current worksheet. You might have some dates and figures that must remain constant, for instance. If that's the case, you can use the Protect Sheet control to establish element-level protection for the worksheet.

1 Click the Review tab.

2 Click the Protect Sheet button.

3 Select the check boxes for the options you want protected in the sheet. If you don't want an option protected, then click the option to clear it.

4 Type a password to prevent users from undoing your protection.

5 Click OK.

6 Retype the password.

7 Click OK.

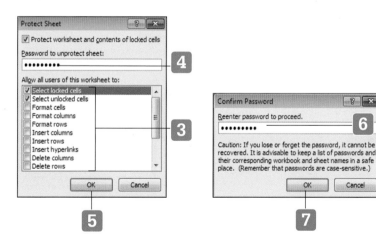

Encrypt a workbook

If you want to take your security up a notch, consider scrambling your password. Actually you can let Excel do the deed through the process of encryption. All you have to do is remember your password.

1 Click the File tab.

2 Click the Protect Workbook button.

3 Select Encrypt with Password from the drop-down list.

4 Type a password.

5 Click OK.

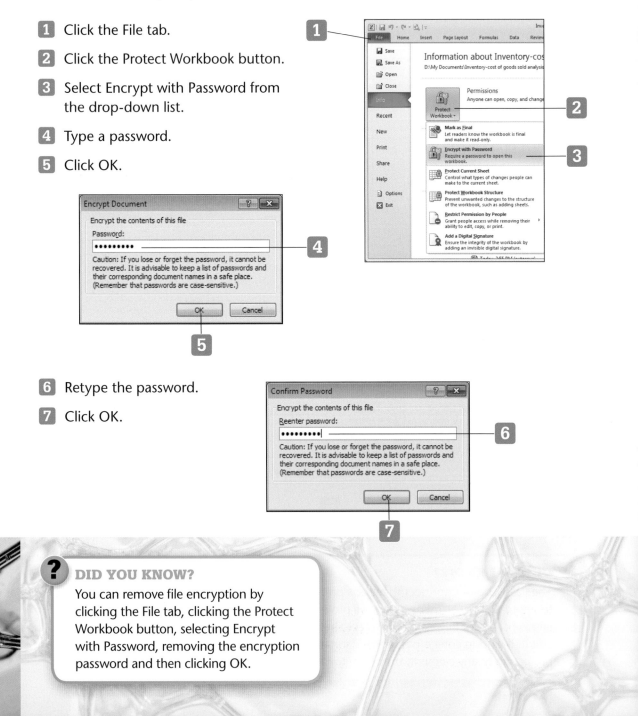

6 Retype the password.

7 Click OK.

? DID YOU KNOW?

You can remove file encryption by clicking the File tab, clicking the Protect Workbook button, selecting Encrypt with Password, removing the encryption password and then clicking OK.

Password protect a workbook

If your workbook is going to move from person to person, a password will make sure that only those who know the password can open it.

1. Select the workbook you want protected.

2. Click the File tab.

3. Click Save As.

4. Click the Tools button, and select General Options.

5. Type a password in the Password to open box or the Password to modify box.

6. Select the Always create backup check box to create a backup. Otherwise click to clear it.

7. Select the Read-only recommended check box to denote the workbook as read-only. Otherwise, click to clear it.

8. Click OK.

9. Retype the password.

10. Click OK and then Save.

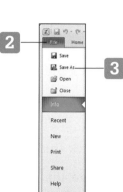

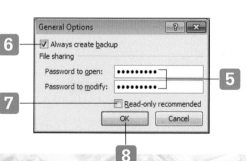

Set add-in security options

An add-in is a great way to customise your ribbon. However, hackers can use this added software code to do bad things such as spreading a virus. By setting security options, you can make sure your add-ins are safe.

1. Click the File tab.

2. Click Options. The Excel Options dialogue box appears.

3. Click Trust Center.

4. Click the Trust Center Settings button. The Trust Center dialogue box appears.

5. Click Add-ins.

6. Select the check boxes to the options you want. Otherwise, click to clear the options.

7. Click OK twice.

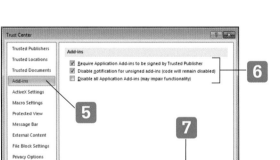

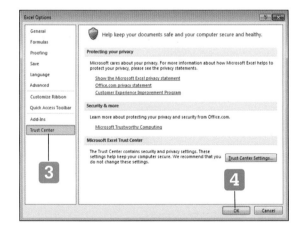

? DID YOU KNOW?

If the add-in security options are not set to the level you need, you can change them in the Trust Center.

Add a digital signature

An artist signs a painting, so you might want to add an invisible digital signature to your workbook. It's a way to prove your identity by providing a stamp of authentication.

1 Click the File tab.

2 Click the Protect Workbook button.

3 Select Add a Digital Signature from the drop-down list.

4 Click OK.

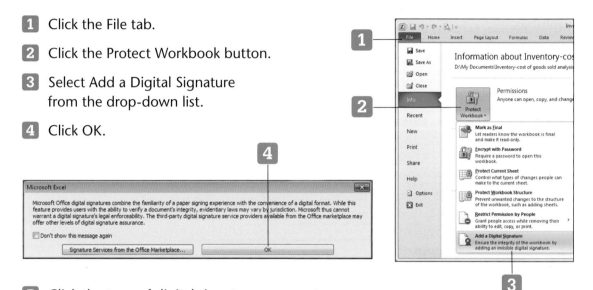

5 Click the type of digital signature you want.

6 Click OK.

7 Follow the steps shown on the Microsoft Office Online site to obtain your digital ID.

🔥 HOT TIP: If you're not sure whether or not a workbook is digitally signed, you can use the Signatures task pane to view or remove signatures.

❓ DID YOU KNOW?

Before you can add a digital signature, you need to get a digital ID or digital certificate. This will provide an electronic way to prove your identity.

View a digital signature

Whether you create a signature or you open a workbook that includes someone else's signature, it's a good idea to take a look at the digital file and understand what you are looking at. That way, you can be sure the signature is genuine and the workbook is reliable.

1 Open the file that contains the digital signature that you want to view.

2 Click the File tab.

3 Click Info and then select View Signatures.
The Signatures pane appears.

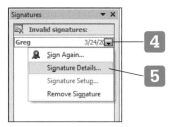

4 In the Signature pane, click the down arrow on the signature.

5 Select Signature Details. The Signature Details dialogue box appears.

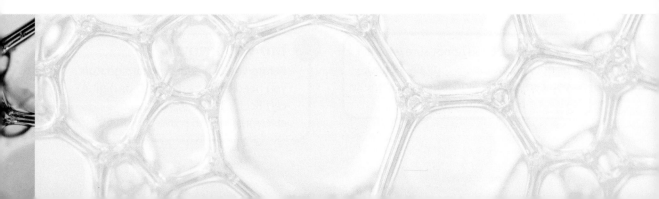

6 In the Signature Details dialogue box, click the View button.

Signature Details

⚠ Invalid signature - The signed content or the signature has been modified.

Purpose for signing this document:

Maintain privacy of sensitive data

Signing as: Greg   View... ── **6**

See the additional signing information
that was collected...   Close ── **8**

7 In the Certificate dialogue box, click OK when you have finished viewing the certificate details.

8 Click Close.

Certificate

General | Details

Certificate Information

This certificate is intended for the following purpose(s):
- All issuance policies
- All application policies

Issued to: Greg

Issued by: Greg

Valid from 3/ 24/ 2010 **to** 3/ 24/ 2011

Issuer Statement

Learn more about certificates

OK ── **7**

? **DID YOU KNOW?**

Invalid digital signatures are indicated by red text in the Signatures pane and a red X on the Signature Details dialogue box.

Adjust message bar security options

You now have the option of having a message bar appear below your ribbon when a potential problem arises. When potentially unsafe content is detected in an open document, it will provide a security warning and give options to enable external content or leave it blocked.

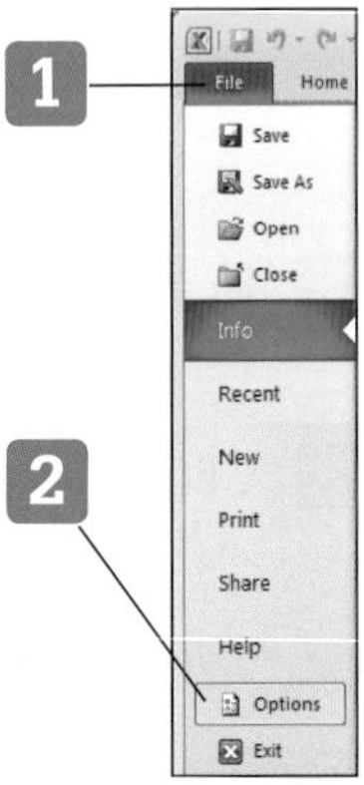

1. Click the File tab.
2. Click Options.
3. In the Excel Options dialogue box, click Trust Center.
4. Click the Trust Center Settings button.

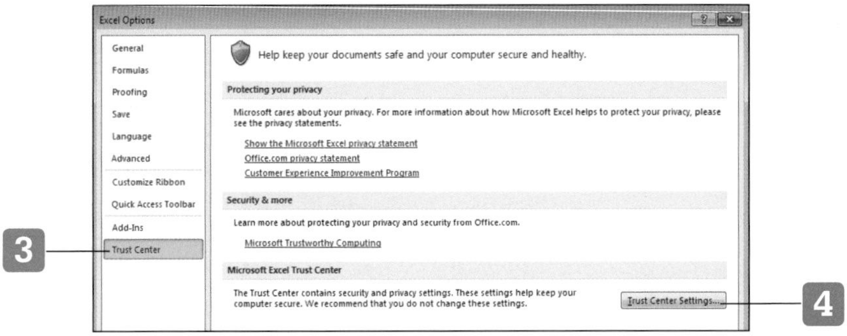

5. In the Trust Center dialogue box, click Message Bar.
6. Click the option you want for showing the Message Bar.
7. Click OK twice.

DID YOU KNOW?

If you do not want to receive alerts about security issues, you can disable the message bar.

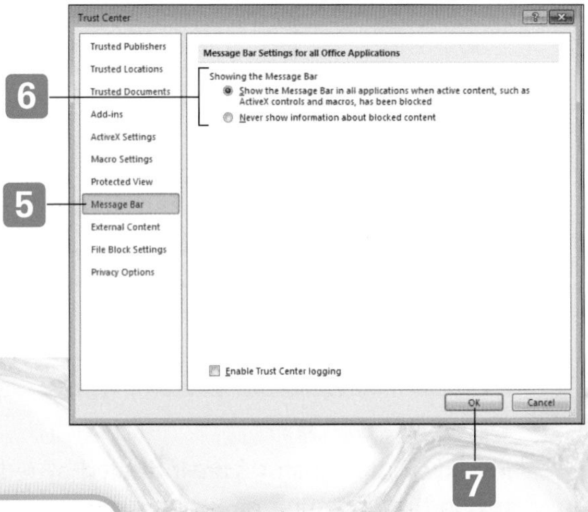

Set privacy options

In this day and age, you can't be too careful about privacy issues. Excel allows you to head trouble off at the pass by protecting you from phishing schemes and making sure your children don't visit websites with offensive content.

1 Click the File tab.

2 Click Options.

3 Click the Trust Center button.

4 Click the Trust Center Settings button.

5 Click Privacy Options.

6 Select the check boxes to the options you want. Otherwise, click to clear them.

7 Click OK twice.

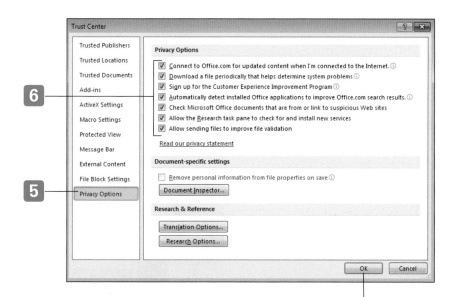

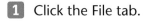

? DID YOU KNOW?

These options can also keep you up to date on such new features as headlines and templates as well as give you help when you need it.

Make a workbook read-only

Making a workbook read-only is a good way to prevent readers and reviewers from making accidental changes. When you use the Mark as Final command, you disable or turn off typing, editing commands and proofing marks. You also set the Status property field in the Document Information Panel to final.

1 Click the File tab.

2 Click Info and then click Protect Workbook.

3 Select Mark as Final from the drop-down list.

4 Click OK.

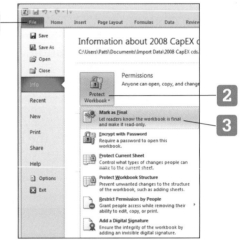

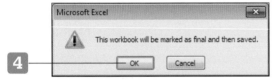

5 If prompted, click OK to confirm that the document has been marked as final and editing is complete.

? DID YOU KNOW?

You'll know you're all set when the Mark as Final icon appears in the status bar. That means your workbook is currently marked as final.

? DID YOU KNOW?

The Mark as Final command is not a security option. It only prevents changes to the workbook while it's turned on. It can be turned off by anyone at any time.

🔥 HOT TIP: If your workbook is marked as final, you can enable editing in a simple way. Just click the File tab, click to Protect Workbook, and then select Mark as Final again to toggle off the Mark as Final feature.

Adjust macro security settings

Macros are convenient, they are sets of commands or steps that you set up and run automatically. Macros have a bad reputation because they can cause virus infections, but the truth is that as long as you have antivirus software running and you take advantage of Office 2010's security features, you should be protected. You can download macros that others have created to help you save time, but make sure you have your trust levels adjusted so you download only macros from reliable sources. Excel's macro settings are listed in Table 9.1.

1 Click the File tab.

2 Click Options.

3 Click Trust Center.

4 Click the Trust Center Settings button.

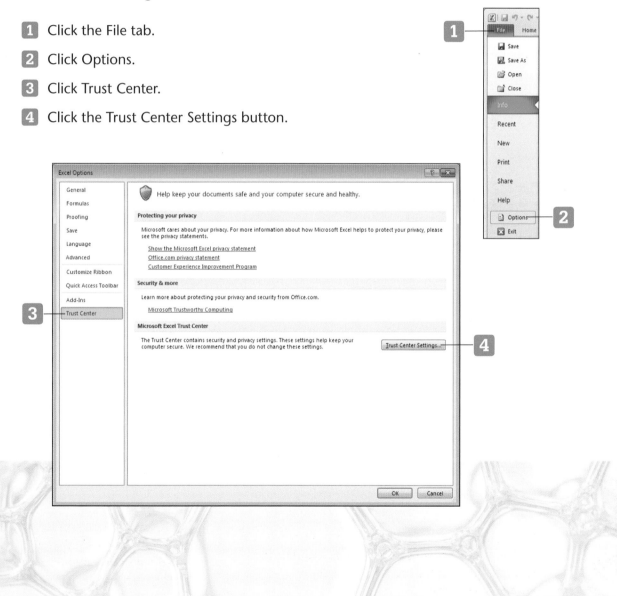

5 Click Macro Settings.

6 Select one of the options that determine how Excel handles macros.

7 Click OK.

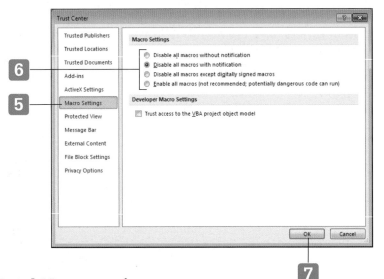

Table 9.1 Excel Macro settings

Setting	What it does
Disable all macros without notification	Blocks all macros; choose this only if you don't want to use any macros
Disable all macros with notification	Macros won't work, but if one is present, you'll see a security alert so you can choose to run it if you wish
Disable all macros except digitally signed macros	If a macro has been 'signed' by a trusted publisher with an encrypted file called a digital signature, Excel runs it automatically
Enable all macros	Excel runs all macros automatically without notifying you and without security protection.

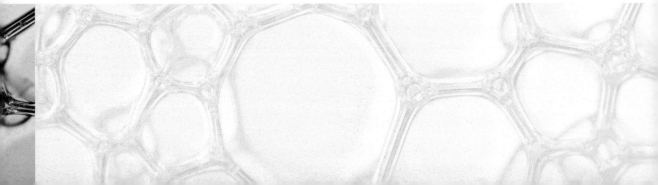

10 Sharing your data with your colleagues

Introduction

In the previous chapter, you learned about the common security options available in Excel 2010. Now you're ready to share your data and collaborate with your colleagues.

Sometimes you're in a work group with colleagues on the other side of the continent. Sometimes you're setting up a budget with your spouse. Sometimes you're exchanging soccer statistics with parents of the other players on your child's team. Instead of dealing with sticky notes on hard-copy outputs, Excel lets you insert electronic comments within worksheet cells. Changes can be tracked. And then they can be sent to another person for review using email or an Internet fax service.

By using a variety of techniques, you can link, embed, hyperlink, export or convert data to create one seamless workbook that is a group effort. You can also use Excel to create and edit connections to external data sources, such as Microsoft Access, to create more permanent links to data.

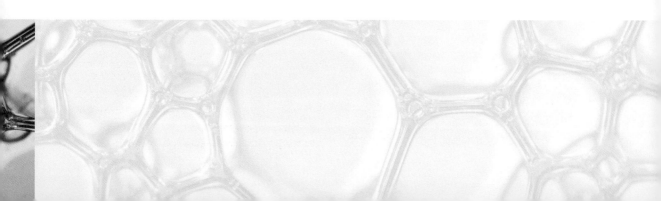

Share a worksheet

Collaboration takes on a new meaning when a group of people have equal responsibility for data within a single workbook. Sharing the Excel way means users can add columns and rows, enter data and change formatting.

1 Open the workbook you want to share.

2 Click the Review tab.

3 Click the Share Workbook button.

4 In the Share Workbook dialogue box, click the Editing tab.

5 Select the Allow changes by more than one user at the same time check box.

6 Click OK.

7 Click OK again to save your workbook.

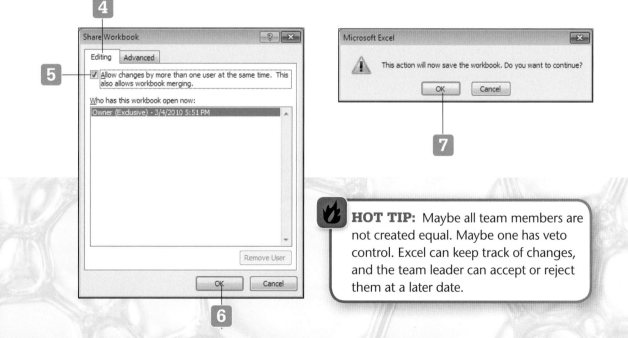

HOT TIP: Maybe all team members are not created equal. Maybe one has veto control. Excel can keep track of changes, and the team leader can accept or reject them at a later date.

Configure sharing options

Simply sharing a file isn't always enough. You may also need to control how long to maintain changes other users make, and to specify how long their changes should be saved. You can do so by configuring sharing options.

1 Open the workbook you want to share.

2 Click the Review tab.

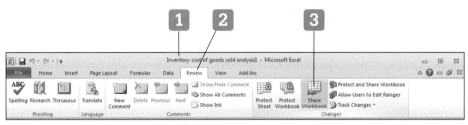

3 Click Share Workbook.

4 In the Share Workbook dialogue box, click the Advanced tab.

5 Select a Track changes option for how long to keep changes, in days.

6 Select an Update changes option for when changes should be made.

7 Click OK.

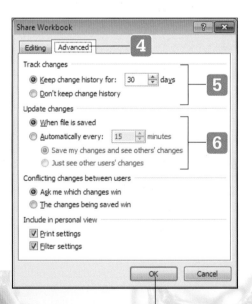

? DID YOU KNOW?

You can also choose an option for Conflicting changes between users to resolve conflicts between changes made by shared users.

Create a cell comment

A comment in Excel is the equivalent of leaving a message to yourself on your answering machine. Or it could be like the to-do list your partner helpfully tapes to the refrigerator door. To create a comment:

1 Click the cell to which you want to add a comment.

2 Click the Review tab.

3 Click the New Comment button.

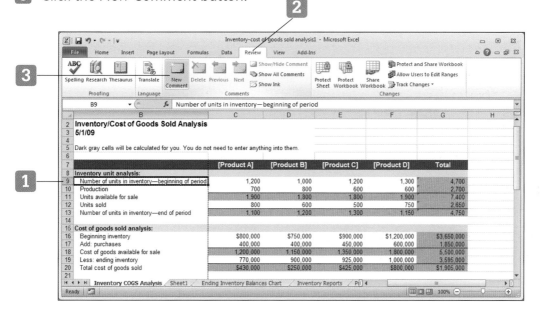

4 Type the comment in the comment box.

5 Click outside the comment box when you are finished, or press Esc twice to close the comment box.

? DID YOU KNOW?

By default, comments are hidden. They are only shown when the mouse pointer hovers over a cell with a red triangle.

Read a comment

A comment is like a sticky note attached to a file. But you have to know how to find comments and how to read them in order to take advantage of them.

1 Position the mouse pointer over a cell with a red triangle to read its comment.

2 Move the mouse pointer off the cell to hide the comment.

3 Click the Review tab.

4 Select a comment option you prefer.

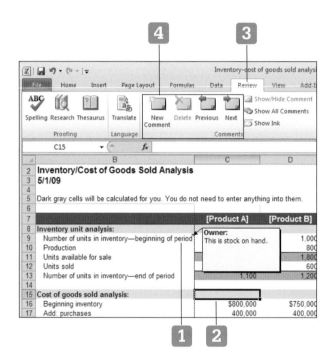

Edit a cell comment

Comments are just like any other text on a worksheet. You can edit or even format them so they stand out from the surrounding comments.

1 Click the cell with the comment you want to edit.

2 Click the Review tab.

3 Click the Edit Comment button.

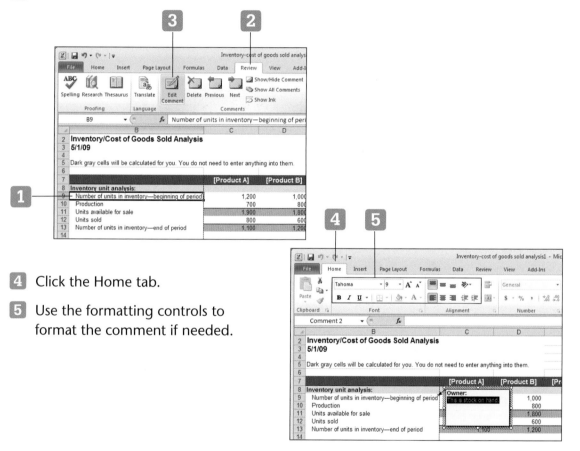

4 Click the Home tab.

5 Use the formatting controls to format the comment if needed.

HOT TIP: If you are editing, you can use common tools (e.g. the Backspace and Delete keys), as well as the Formatting toolbar buttons. Then press Esc twice to close the comment box.

Track changes

Anyone who writes knows that the finished product may have little resemblance to the original version or even to the multiple drafts. They key is usually not to edit as you go along but put everything in and then hone it at the end. The Track Changes feature of Excel makes it possible to see who made what changes when, and decide later which to keep or reject.

1 Click the Review tab.

2 Click the Track Changes button, and then select Highlight Changes from the drop-down list.

? DID YOU KNOW?

Column and row indicators for changed cells appear in red. The cell containing the changes has a blue outline. Changes can be viewed by moving your mouse pointer over any outlined cell.

3 Select the Track changes while editing check box.

4 Select the When, Who and/or Where check boxes. Select an option that you want from the associated list.

5 Select the Highlight changes on screen or List changes on a new sheet check boxes. Otherwise, click to clear them.

6 Click OK and then click OK again if necessary.

7 Make changes in worksheet cells.

8 To view tracked changes, position the mouse pointer over an edited cell.

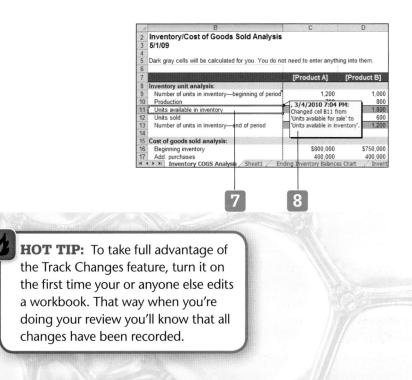

HOT TIP: To take full advantage of the Track Changes feature, turn it on the first time your or anyone else edits a workbook. That way when you're doing your review you'll know that all changes have been recorded.

Review tracked changes

Once you activate track changes for a document, you and your colleagues can take full advantage of it by moving from one change to another and accepting it or rejecting it.

1 Click the Review tab.

2 Click Track Changes and then click Accept/Reject Changes.

3 Change tracking, if needed, and click OK to start reviewing changes.

4 Select Accept, Reject, Accept All or Reject All.

5 Click Close.

? **DID YOU KNOW?**

When you or anyone else applies the Track Changes command to a workbook, the message '[Shared]' appears in the title bar of the workbook. That way you know that this feature is active.

Email a workbook for review

When your workbook is ready to show, you don't have to take it on the road. You don't even have to open your regular email program. Excel allows you send your workbook to others for review as an attachment, as a workbook, PDF or XPS document. Your reviewer can use the same procedure to send your workbook back to you when they have completed their comments.

1 Click the File tab.

2 Click Share.

3 Select Send Using E-mail.

4 Select Send as Attachment, Send a Link, Send as PDF, Send as XPS or Send as Internet Fax.

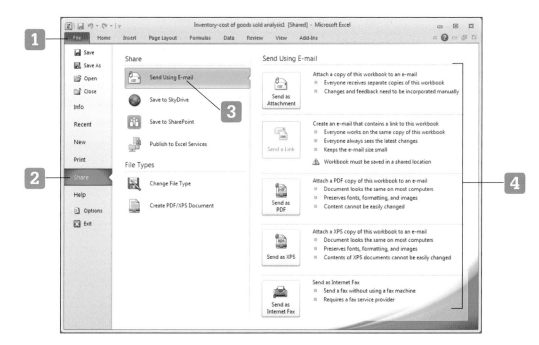

An email program, such as Microsoft Outlook, needs to be installed on your computer and your email account needs to be set up. A Compatibility Checker will appear, and you'll need to click Continue or Cancel to stop the operation.

5 Enter email addresses or select users from your Address Book.

6 Enter a message for your reviewer with instructions.

7 Click the Send button.

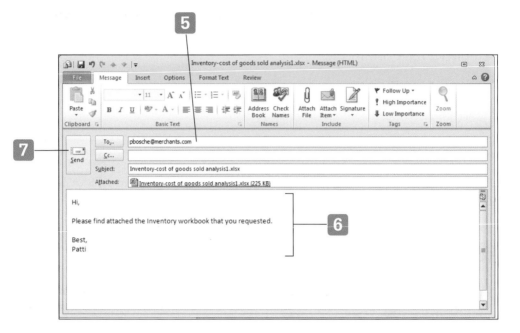

HOT TIP: To add recipients from your address book or contacts list, click To, click the recipients' names, click To, Cc or Bcc until you're done, and then click OK.

Work with XML

Excel is a great program, but in some cases it might be helpful to store data independently of its format. That way you can use the data more seamlessly in other forms. XML is short for Extensible Markup Language, and it's your new best friend.

1 Click the Developer tab.

2 Click the Source button.

3 In the task pane, click the XML Maps button.

4 Click Add.

HOT TIP: To change your XML view options, go to the XML Source task pane. Click Options to turn on or off options to preview data in the task pane, hide help text in the task pane, automatically merge elements when mapping, include data headings, or hide the borders of inactive lists.

5 Locate and select the XML schema file you want to attach, and then click Open. If prompted, click OK to create a schema based on the XML source data.

6 To delete or rename an XML schema, click XML Maps.

7 Select the schema from the list.

8 If you delete the XML schema, click Delete and then click OK when prompted. If you rename to XML schema, click Rename.

9 Click OK.

10 When you're done, click the Close button on the task pane.

Change XML properties

You won't need to know the XML language to attach an XML schema. Just remember that an XML schema is a set of rules that defines the elements and content used in an XML document. And you can change the XML properties of any file before you attach or export it.

1 Click the Developer tab.

2 Click the Source button.

3 Click Map Properties.

4 Rename the map if you wish.

5 Change the map options.

6 Specify the refreshing or importing data option you want.

7 Click OK.

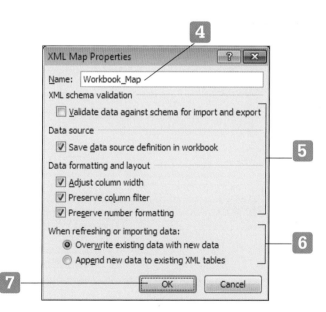

? **DID YOU KNOW?**

When you add an XML map to a workbook, Microsoft Office Excel 2010 provides default XML map names in the following way: Workbook_Map, Workbook_Map1, Workbook_Map2, and so on. To avoid confusion, you may want to provide more meaningful names to the XML map, especially if you are working with more than one XML map.

Export data in XML

Once you finish formatting your XML file, you can export or save the data for use in other XML compatible applications.

1 Open the worksheet that contains the data you want to export.

2 Click the Developer tab.

3 Click the Source button.

4 Click Export.

5 Browse to the location where you want to save the XML file.

6 Click Export.

? DID YOU KNOW?

The XML data format is an industry standard that uses its own XML schema, while the XML spreadsheet format is a specialised XML file that uses its own XML schema.

Export data

Let's say that there is text in another file that you want to include in your worksheet. Importing allows you to open that text file in your workbook. Or if you want to copy data from one program to another, you can convert the data to a format that the other program accepts. To export an Excel file to another program format, follow these steps:

1 Open the file from which you want to export data.

2 Click the File tab.

3 Click Save As.

4 Click the Save in list arrow, and then click the drive or folder where you want to save the file.

5 Click the Save as type list arrow, and then click the format you want. If you want to change the file name, do it now.

6 Click Save.

Import a text file

You can also import text you want to include in your worksheet. Rather than scrolling across the text and using cutting and pasting, it can be more efficient to simply import the entire text file.

1 Click the File tab.

2 Click Open.

3 Click the Look in list arrow, and then select the folder where the text file name is located.

4 Click the Files of type list arrow, and then click Text Files.

5 Select the text file you want to import.

6 Click Open.

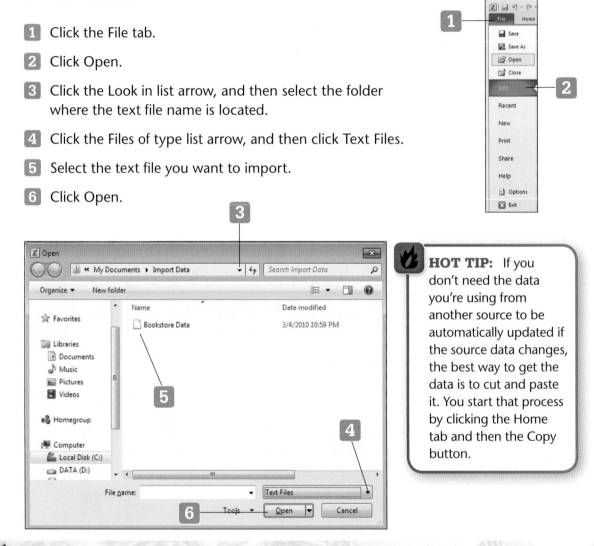

HOT TIP: If you don't need the data you're using from another source to be automatically updated if the source data changes, the best way to get the data is to cut and paste it. You start that process by clicking the Home tab and then the Copy button.

? DID YOU KNOW?

When you're importing a text file (.txt), Excel starts the Import Text Wizard automatically.

? DID YOU KNOW?

Excel can save a file to a format only with an installed converter. If your format doesn't appear in the Save as type list, you'll need to install it by running Setup from the Microsoft Office 2010 CD.

Link data

If you have a number of sets of data that are the same, resist the urge to make multiple identical entries. Instead, links are the way to go. That way you'll save time and make sure your entries are correct.

1 Select the cell or range that contains the source data.

2 Click the Home tab.

3 Click the Copy button.

4 Click the sheet tab where you want to link the data.

5 Select the destination cell or destination range.

6 Click the Paste button.

7 Click the Paste Options button, and then select Paste Link.

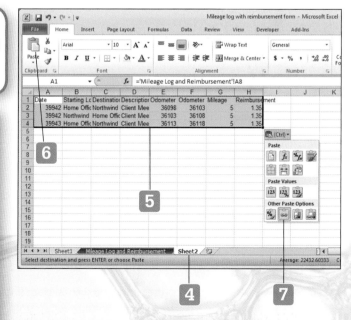

HOT TIP: To arrange open worksheet windows to make linking easier, click the View tab, and then click the Arrange All button.

DID YOU KNOW?

A link can be as simple as a reference to a cell on another worksheet, or it can be part of a formula. You can link cells between sheets within one workbook or between different workbooks. Cell data to be linked is called the source data. The cell or range linked to the source data is called the destination cell or destination range. If you no longer want linked data to be updated, you can easily break a link.

Get external data

The Data Connection Wizard connects to an external data source that has already been established. It's a good way to create a permanent exchange to a data source if you're going to be using it regularly.

1 Click the Data tab.

2 Click the From Other Sources button.

3 Click From Data Connection Wizard.

Manage connections

It's good up to a point to be able to use your connection file for sharing connections with other users. But if you change your connection information, your connection file will not be updated automatically.

1 Click the Data tab.

2 Click the Connections button.

3 In the Workbook Connections dialogue box, click the Add button.

4 Click the Show list arrow, and then click All Connections or select the specific connection type you want to display.

5 Click Open.

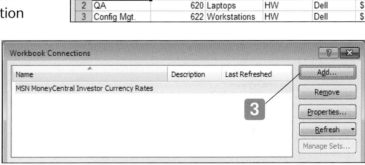

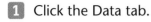

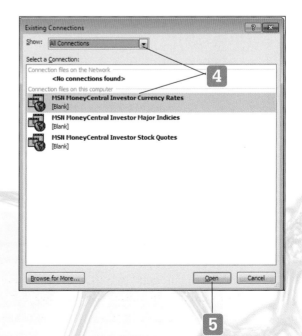

? DID YOU KNOW?

You can use the Connection Properties dialogue box to set options for connections to external data sources, as well as to use, reuse or switch connection files.

Top 10 Excel 2010 Problems Solved

Problem 1: Excel isn't working properly. What can I do to fix it?

If you find that Excel isn't operating properly, the first line of defence is to use the Office Diagnostics application. Use it if you see an alert message or other indications that Excel can't find data, is running slowly or is experiencing mix-ups with data stored in the Windows registry.

1 Click Start and then click Control Panel.

2 Click Programs.

3 Click Programs and Features.

4 From the Uninstall or change a program dialogue box, select your version of Microsoft Office 2010.

5 Click Change.

6 Click the Repair option.

7 Click Continue. The repair process may take some time.

8 When the process completes, you will need to restart your computer for the changes to take effect. Click Close.

9 Click either Yes to restart your computer now or click No to restart your computer later.

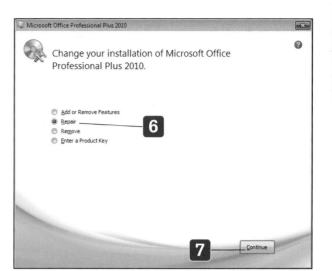

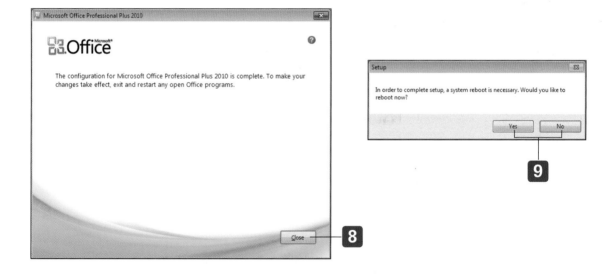

? DID YOU KNOW?

Diagnostic information gathered from your computer is compiled and kept on your computer. When Office Diagnostics determines that the data might help diagnose and fix a problem, the system asks whether you want to send the information to Microsoft. After the tests are completed, you are prompted to visit a webpage to get advice based the results of the tests.

Problem 2: How do I enable Save Mode?

You might be familiar with Safe Mode from problems with the Windows operating system: if the system encounters a serious problem, you have the option of starting in Safe Mode to repair it. Excel and other Office applications also switch to Safe Mode when they encounter major difficulties. In fact, Office uses two types of Safe Mode: Automated and User-Initiated. If an Office program is not able to start up after encountering problems, it automatically starts in Safe Mode the next time you try to use it. But you may need to manually enable Safe Mode yourself to make this option available.

1 Click the File tab.

2 Select Options.

3 Click Trust Center.

4 Click the Trust Center Settings button.

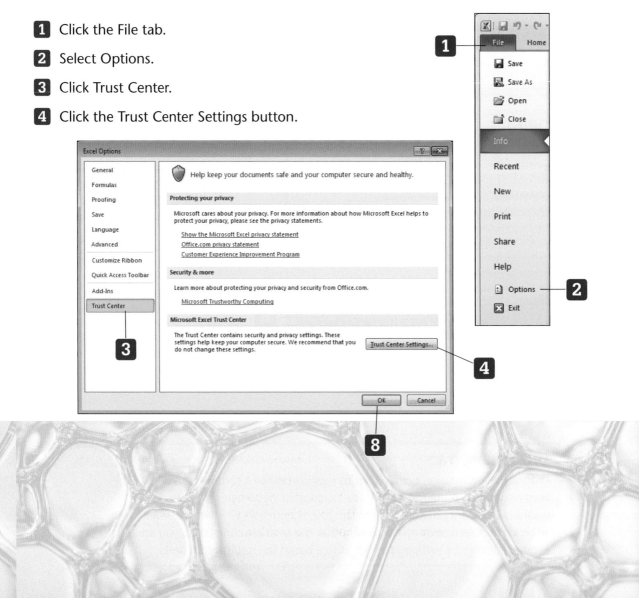

5 Click ActiveX Settings.

6 Select the Safe Mode check box.

7 Click OK.

8 Click OK.

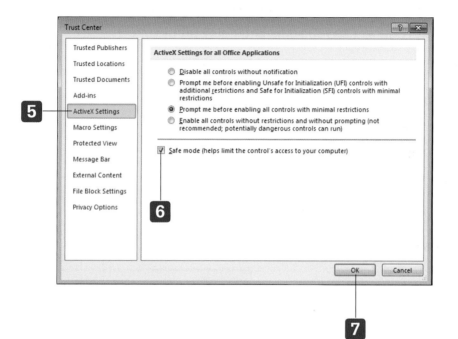

Problem 3: How do I correct an Excel formula?

Formulas in Excel can quickly become complicated, but tools are available to help you track down problems. One, the Watch Window, keeps track of cells you specify. If you make changes to a worksheet that affect the cells and any formulas associated with them, the Watch Window lets you know about any problems.

1 Open the worksheet you want to monitor, and select the cells you want to watch.

2 Click the Formulas tab.

3 Click the Watch Window button.

4 In the Watch Window dialogue box, click the Add Watch button.

5 Select the cells you want to watch, and click Add.

6 Click Close.

HOT TIP: To select all of a worksheet's cells at once, click the button in the upper left-hand corner, which simply has an arrow pointing down and to the right. Otherwise click and drag over cells to select them.

Problem 4: I can't send my workbook via email. What can I do?

Excel normally gives you the ability to send a workbook to someone else via email, as long as your computer is connected to the Internet or a local computer network. It can happen that, when you point to the Send command on the Office menu, you discover either that the Send command is unavailable or the email option is missing. The cause may be that Microsoft Outlook is not designated as your default email program.

1 Start Microsoft Internet Explorer by selecting it from the Start menu or the taskbar.

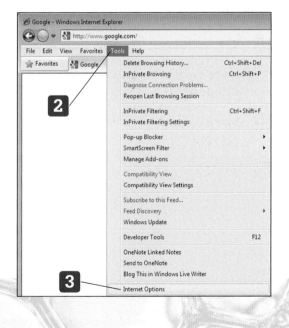

2 From the menu bar, click Tools.

3 Select Internet Options.

4 Click the Programs tab.

5 Click Set programs.

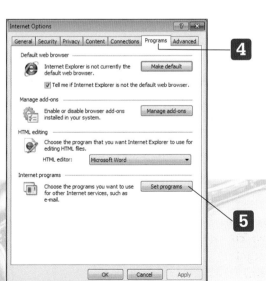

6 Click Set your default programs.

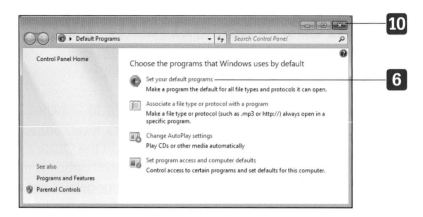

7 Select your default program from the left pane.

8 Click Set this program as default.

9 Click OK.

10 Close the dialogue box.

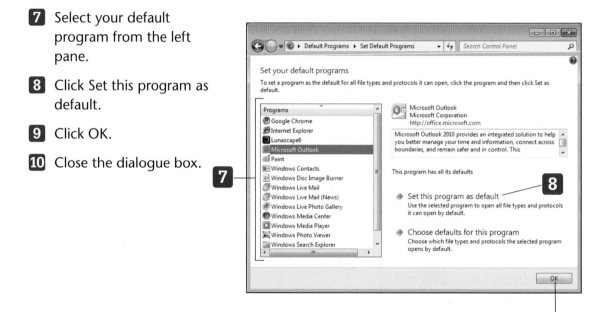

? DID YOU KNOW?

You can always send the file as an attachment using your default email program until you select Outlook as your default email application.

Problem 5: How do I check an Excel worksheet for errors?

The Error Checker is another automated feature that tracks any errors in your worksheet formulas. It follows rules that apply to formula preparation to uncover problems. The Error Checker works in the background while you edit your worksheet.

1 Open the worksheet you want to check for errors.

2 Click the Formulas tab.

3 Click the Error Checking button.

4 Select Error Checking from the drop-down list. Click Resume if needed. The Error Checker automatically scans the worksheet for errors.

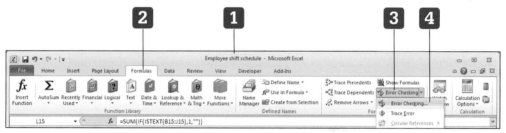

5 If an error is found, select the Help on this error button or one of the other buttons to handle the error.

6 Click the Options button to change the options related to formula calculations, performance and error handling.

7 Click Previous or Next to proceed with the check. When you're done, click Close.

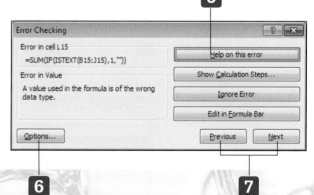

? DID YOU KNOW?

You can specify error checking options before you use the Error Checker. Click the File tab, click Options, click Formulas, and tick the Enable background error checking box. Select the error checking rule check boxes you want, and then click OK.

Problem 6: How do I remove comments from worksheets?

Comments are textual notes that coworkers are able to add to Excel worksheets. When it is time to print a document or email it to others for review, you'll need to strip out the comments first.

1 Click the Home tab.

2 Click the Find & Select button.

3 Select Comments from the drop-down list. All comments in the current worksheet with comments are selected.

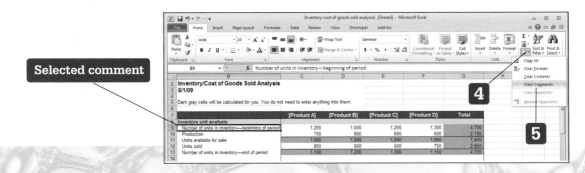

4 Click Clear.

5 Select Clear Comments from the drop-down list to remove all comments.

Selected comment

DID YOU KNOW?

If you need to remove comments from an entire workbook, click Office, point to Prepare and select Inspect document. Untick all boxes except Comments and Annotations. Click Inspect. If comments are found, click Remove All and then click Close.

Problem 7: I need to adjust a formula, how do I evaluate it first?

When you created a nested formula, it can be difficult to determine exactly how Excel performs the necessary calculations if you need to adjust or correct them. The Evaluate Formula dialogue box helps you evaluate parts of a formula one at a time.

1 Select the cell that contains the formula you want to evaluate.

2 Click the Formulas tab.

3 Click Evaluate Formula.

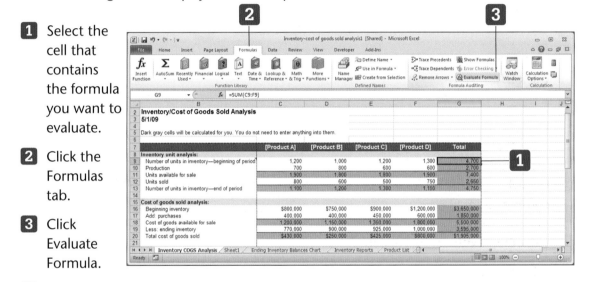

4 Click the Evaluate button to examine the value of the reference.

5 Continue until each part of the formula has been evaluated, and then click Close.

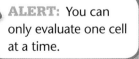 **ALERT:** You can only evaluate one cell at a time.

Problem 8: How do I find a missing add-in?

Add-ins are additional programs that are designed to run within Excel and perform specialised functions. Sometimes, functions aren't available because the add-in needed to run them cannot be found. If that's the case, you have several troubleshooting options.

1 From the quick access toolbar, click the Add-Ins button.

2 Select the check boxes for the add-ins you want to use.

3 Click OK.

4 To check for other add-ins you have available, click the File tab.

5 Select Options.

6 Click Add-Ins.

7 Select the add-in to display details about it.

8 Click OK.

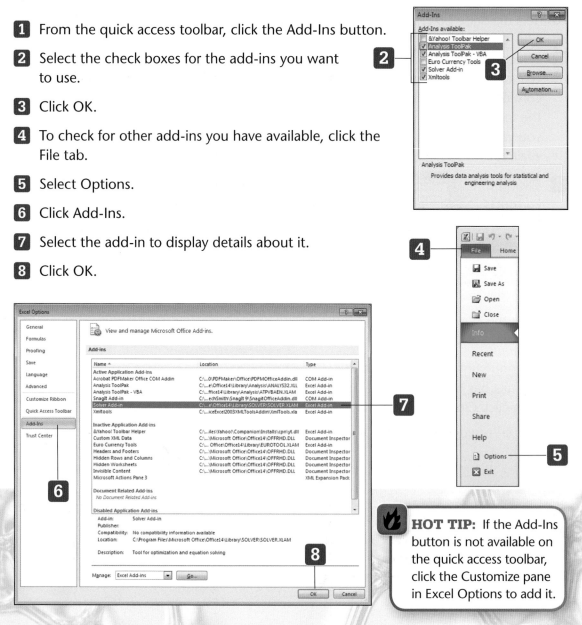

> **HOT TIP:** If the Add-Ins button is not available on the quick access toolbar, click the Customize pane in Excel Options to add it.

Problem 9: How do I troubleshoot invalid data?

Data Validation enables you to ensure that data has been entered in the format you want. The rules you configure to validate data check the information, and you can tell Excel to highlight data that violates the rules (invalid data) so you can make corrections.

1 Click the Data tab.

2 Click Data Validation.

3 Select Circle Invalid Data from the drop-down list. Red circles appear around cells that contain invalid data.

4 To clear the circles, select Data Validation again.

5 Select Clear Validation Circles from the drop-down list.

> ▶ **SEE ALSO:** See 'Create a drop-down list' in Chapter 6 for an example of adding validation rules to one type of object in a worksheet.

Problem 10: How do I ensure that Excel opens and displays a workbook?

In certain circumstances, you might double-click a workbook file to open it and, instead of displaying the selected file, Excel opens without displaying any file. Instead you see an error message such as 'Windows cannot find *Filepath\Filename*, Make sure you typed the name correctly, and then try again'. A possible cause is that Ignore other applications is selected as an Excel option.

1 Click the File button.

2 Select Options.

3 Click Advanced.

4 Scroll down to the General section, and clear the Ignore other applications check box to clear it.

5 Click OK.

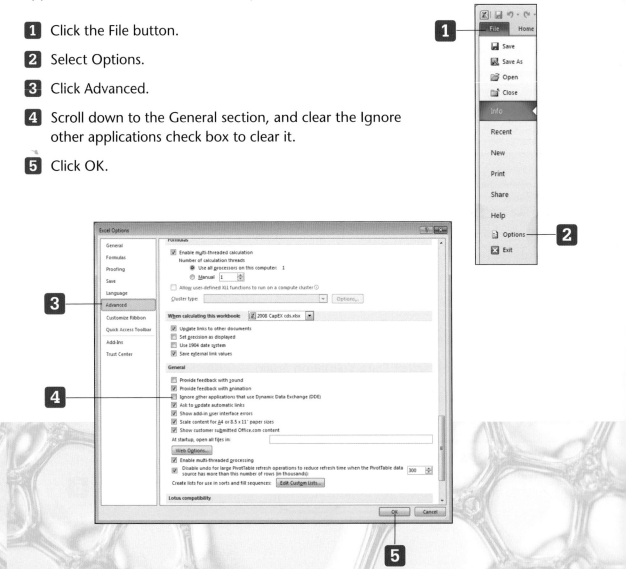